Dreams in Homespun

By Sam Walter Foss

PANTIANOS
CLASSICS

Published by Pantianos Classics

ISBN-13: 978-1-78987-080-0

First published in 1897

They beckon you forth in wide spaces,
  To a lifted and far-shining goal,
To a new federation of races
  And a fatherland fit for the soul
                Sam Walter Foss

Contents

To My Brother and Sister, Clarence and Ethel Foss

Ah, let us rest beneath the trees,
*   Nor seek with an adventurous prow*
The magic isles of distant seas,
*   But sing the Songs of Here and Now.*
The world has long been sailed around.
And El Dorado's still unfound;
The quest is vain on many seas
For apples of Hesperides;
And in no land of woods and flowers
Doth Norumbega lift its towers;
And in the sunset-mantled west
There are no Islands of the Blest.
But there is magic in the near.
*   And beauty blooms on every bough;*
And there are Hesper islands here.
*   And there are El Dorados now.*

The seas are wide the swift ships plough,
*   And long is the Platonic year;*
But all the best of time is now.
*   And all the best of space is here.*
A trace of Eden still must be
Where blooms a rose or grows a tree;
And Paphian glories wander by
The man who gazes on the sky;
The Isles of Peace, the Seats of Rest,
Are not in islands of the west;
The Golden Age that knew no tears
Is not within the vanished years;
Not far the Golden Age, but near;
*   Fate's fruit is on the nearest bough, -*
So sing the Songs of Now and Here,
*   The brave, glad Songs of Here and Now,*

The Town of Hay

The town of Hay is far away.
    The town of Hay is far;
Between its hills of green and gray
    Its winding meadows are.
Within the quiet town of Hay
    Is many a quiet glen,
And there by many a shaded way
Are homes of quiet men:
        And there are many hearts alway
        That turn with longing, night and day,
            Back to the town of Hay.

Within that good old town of Hay
    There was no pride of birth.
And no man there pursued his way
    A stranger in the earth;
And none were high and none were low,
    Of golden-hair or gray,
And each would grieve at other's woe
    Down in the town of Hay:
        And many a world-scorned soul to-day
        Mid crowded thousands far away
            Weeps for the town of Hay.

A road leads from the town of Hay;
    Forth to a world of din,
And winds and wanders far away —
    And many walked therein;
Far in the crowds of toil and stress
    Their restless footsteps stray, —
Their souls have lost the quietness
    Of that old town of Hay:
        But in some respite of the fray,
        In transient dreams they float away,
            Back to the town of Hay.

Old men are in that town of Hay,
    Amid its quiet trees.
Who dream of strong sons far away
    Upon the stormy seas;
Old mothers, when the twilight dew

8

The woodbine leaves have pearled,
Dream of their boys who wander through
　　The wideness of the world:
　　　　And tears fall in the twilight gray,
　　　　And prayers go up at close of day
　　　　　In that old town of Hay.

A hillside in the town of Hay
　　Is slanting toward the sun,
And gathered 'neath its headstones gray
　　Are sleepers, one by one;
And there are tears in distant lands.
　　And grief too deep for tears.
And farewells waved from phantom hands
　　Across the gulf of years:
　　　　And when they place that headstone gray,
　　　　It crushes hearts so far away
　　　　　From that old town of Hay.

Aunt Haskett

I

He had a big house, an' a fine, tall house,
　　An' there ain't no house no bigger;
An his lawn roun' his house was as big as a farm,
　　An' he cut a tremendous big figger,
An' he had slues er bosses, an' all kinds er rigs,
　　An' a pond that was full er tame fishes;
An' his wife had silk dresses and ribbins an' things,
　　An' slathers, I guess, of gold dishes;
An' he lived out his days an' flew high.
　　As gay as a colt out to grass;
W'en he wanted for pie — he had pie,
　　W'en he wanted for sass — he had sass,
And, w'en he died, they made a big spread.
And all thought a mighty rich feller was dead.

An' his funeral percession strung out for two mile,
　　An' his coffin was kivered 'ith flowers,
An' a pesky fine funeral sermon was preached,
　　An' the programme took all of four hours;
An' the mourners, they all took their han'kerchiefs out,
　　An' they looked jest as if they was cryin'.

9

They tried dreffle hard; an', if most of 'em failed.
    It wa'n't for no lack of hard tryin'.
For they all rubbed their eyes an' looked sad,
    An' the women, they all tried to sob.
An' they all tried their best to feel bad;
    But they foun' it a pooty hard job j
For in spite of his houses an' money an' all
It was hard work to cry at his funeral.

Guess he was a great man an' all that — I dunno;
    Guess he was — I dunno — a big banker.
But for jest sich a sort of a feller like him
    A critter like me doesn't hanker.
For he didn't seem to know that warm heart-blood is red;
    All he knew was that gol' coin is yeller;
An' there warn't no juice in the ol' rascal's heart
    An' there warn't no soul in the feller.
An' so, w'en the ol' critter died.
    There warn't no hullabaloo;
An' his neighbors was all satisfied.
    An' they thought 'twas the right thing to do.
Though his funeral was scrumptious an' stylish an' all.
It was hard work to cry at his funeral.

II

A'nt Haskett, she useter do washin' for him,
    An' bent herself double 'ith workin';
An' she did the job stiddy for thirty-five year,
    An' didn' know the natur' of shirkin'.
An' her ol' hands was as hard as the sole er my boot,
    An' her face was as brown as tanned leather;
But she managed by washin' ten hours a day
    To keep soul an' body together.
So she passed through her life's humble scenes,
    A drudge in the big drudgin' masses;
W'en she wanted for pie — she had beans,
    W'en she wanted for sass — she had 'lasses;
An', w'en she was gone, then we all on us said
That a almighty hard-workin' woman was dead.

She had nursed all her days, w'en her washin' was through.
    Every baby aroun' the hull region,
An' the measles she'd cured in thirty-five year
    Come up purty nigh to a legion.

She was great on lobelyer an' pennyrial tea
    An' a wonder on sassafras bitters;
An' she knew roots an' arbs, an' could bile 'em an' mix
    So's to cure all sick human critters;
An' her funeral was belt in her yard,
    'Cause her house was too small for the crowd.
An' the women, they sobbed, an' sobbed hard;
    An' the men folks, *they* cried, an' cried loud;
An' there warn't no style an' no show-off at all;
But 'twas easy to cry at her funeral.

It was easy enough, an' we didn't have to try;
    We cried in the col' grave to leave her,
For we thought of the times she had stood by our beds
    Through the long crazy nights of the fever;
An' we looked the last time on the ol', wrinkled face
    An' the ol', wrinkled hands in the casket.
An' none thought the Lord's heaven too stylish a place
    For the unwrinkled soul of A'nt Haskett.
She washed for the rich man, — a slave
    To hard work an' to pain an' distress,
But measured by tears at her grave
    Her life was the biggest success.
There warn't no style an' no show-off at all.
But 'twas easy to cry at her funeral.

A Life Story

"He is too young to know it now,
But some day he will know."
— **Eugene Field.**

Above her little sufferer's bed,
    With all a mother's grace,
She stroked the curly, throbbing head,
    And smoothed the fevered face.
"He does not know my love, my fears,
    My toil of heart and hand;
But some day in the after years.
    Some day he'll understand;
        Some day he'll know
        I loved him so;
    Some day he'll understand."
A wild lad plays his thoughtless part
    As fits his childhood's lot.
And tramples on his mother's heart
    Ofttimes and knows it not.

11

He plays among his noisy mates
    Nor knows his truest friend;
His mother sighs, as still she waits:

"Some day he'll comprehend;
    The day will be
    When he will see;
Some day he'll comprehend."

The strong youth plays his strenuous part;
    His mother waits alone;
And soon he finds another heart —
    The mate unto his own.
She gives him up in joy and woe;
    He takes his young bride's hand;
His mother murmurs, "Will he know
    And ever understand?
      When will he know
      I love him so?
    When will he understand?"

The strong man fights his battling days, —
    The fight is hard and grim;
His mother's plain, old-fashioned ways
    Have little charm for him.
The dimness falls around her years,
    The shadows 'round her stand,
She mourns in loneliness and tears:
    "He'll never understand;
      He'll never know
      I loved him so;
    He'll never understand."

A bearded man of serious years
    Bends down above the dead,
And rains the tribute of his tears
    Over an old gray head.
He stands the open grave above,
    Amid the mourning bands:
And now he knows his mother's love
    And now he understands.
      Now doth he know
      She loved him so,
    And now he understands.

The House by The Side of The Road

"He was a friend to man, and lived in a house by the side of the road." — **Homer.**

There are hermit souls that live withdrawn
    In the peace of their self-content;
There are souls, like stars, that dwell apart,
    In a fellowless firmament;
There are pioneer souls that blaze their paths
    Where highways never ran; —
But let me live by the side of the road
    And be a friend to man.

Let me live in a house by the side of the road,
Where the race of men go by —
The men who are good and the men who are bad,
As good and as bad as I.
I would not sit in the scorner's seat.
Or hurl the cynic's ban; —
Let me live in a house by the side of the road
And be a friend to man.

I see from my house by the side of the road.
    By the side of the highway of life.
The men who press with the ardor of hope,
    The men who are faint with the strife.
But I turn not away from their smiles nor their tears —
    Both parts of an infinite plan; —
Let me live in my house by the side of the road
    And be a friend to man.

I know there are brook-gladdened meadows ahead
    And mountains of wearisome height;
That the road passes on through the long afternoon
    And stretches away to the night.
But still I rejoice when the travellers rejoice,
    And weep with the strangers that moan,
Nor live in my house by the side of the road
    Like a man who dwells alone.
Let me live in my house by the side of the road
    Where the race of men go by —
They are good, they are bad, they are weak, they are strong,
Wise, foolish — so am I.
Then why should I sit in the scorner's seat
    Or hurl the cynic's ban? —

Let me live in my house by the side of the road
    And be a friend to man.

The Ghost of John Gear

In his coffin bed John Gear lay dead,
    But John Gear's ghost stood near;
And the clergyman talked at the funeral,
    And the Ghost bent low to hear:
The waiting ghost of the man who was dead,
He lingered to hear what the clergyman said;
So the clergyman spake and the people wept,
And the Ghost looked on and the dead man slept
            And the dead man slept.

"The man who is dead," the clergyman said,
    "Was the true, true salt of the earth;
Who shall gauge the good of his well-spent life
    And the measure of his worth?
For he was a man of the olden type.
Of the honest, noble, sterling stripe."
Shame fell on the Ghost as he stood nigh,
For he alone knew these words were a lie —
            These words were a lie.

And the Ghost was afraid and was sore dismayed
    As he heard the words of praise;
And he thought of the wreck and the wrong he had done
    Through the stretch of the long- gone days;
And a woman's face that was blanched with tears
Loomed up from the vast of the clamoring years;
But the Ghost, while he heard all the praise of the priest,
Felt burn on his forehead the mark of the Beast —
            The mark of the Beast.

And the priest preached on, but the ghost of John
    Heard naught but the woman's tears;
For the silent tears of her silent life
    Were thunder in his ears.
And the priest still preached with his words of praise,
And the Face loomed up from the long-gone days;
The priest still praised and the people wept,
And the Ghost passed on and the dead man slept —
            The dead man slept.

14

A Modern Martyrdom

The Weverwend Awthur Murway Gween,
    They say is verwy clevah;
And sister Wuth could heah him pweach,
    Fohevah and fohevah.
And I went down to heah him pweach,
    With Wuth and my Annette,
Upon the bwave, hewoic deaths
    The ancient mawtahs met;
And as he wepwesented them,
    In all their acts and feachaws.
The ancient mawtahs, dontcherknow?
    Were doocid clevah cweachaws.

But, aw deah me! They don't compah
    In twue hewoic bwavewy.
To a bwave he wo fwiend of mine,
    Young Montmowenci Averwy.
He earned foah dollahs everwy week,
    And not anothah coppah;
But this bwave soul wesolved to dwess
    Pwe-eminently pwoppah.
So this was all the food each day,
    The bwave young cweachaw had —
One glaws of milk, a cigawette,
    Foah rwackers, and some bwead.

He lived on foahteen cents a day,
    And cherwished one gweat passion:
The pwecious pwoject of his soul.
    Of being dwessed in fashion.
But when he'd earned a suit entiah,
    To his supweme chagwln,
Just then did shawt-tailed coats go out,
    And long-tailed coats come in;
But naught could bweak his wigid will,
    And now, I pway you, note.
That he gave up his glaws of milk
    And bought a long-tailed coat.

But then the fashion changed once moah.
    And bwought a gwievous plight;
It changed from twousers that are loose

To twousers that are tight.
Then his foah cwackers he gave up.
    He just wenounced their use;
And changed to twousers that are tight,
    Fwom twousers that are loose.
And then the narwow-toed style shoes
    To bwoad-toed changed instead;
Then he pwocured a bwoad-toed paih,
    And gave up eating bwead.

Just then the bwoad-bwimmed style of hat
    To narwow bwims gave way;
And so his twibulations gwew,
    Incweasing everwy day.
But he pwocured a narwow bwim,
    Of verwy stylish set;
But, bwave, bwave soul! he had to dwop
    His pwecious cigawette.
But now when his whole suit confohmed
    To fashion's wegulation,
For lack of cwackers, milk, and bwead.
    He perwished of stahvation.

Thus in his owah of victowy,
    He passed on to his west —
I weally nevah saw a cawpse
    So fashionably dwessed.
My teahs above his well-dwessed clay
    Fell like the spwingtime wains;
My eyes had nevah wested on
    Such pwoppah dwessed remains.
The ancient mawtahs — they were gwand
    And glowious in their day;
But this bwave Montmowenci was
    As gweat and gwand as they.

The Zeitgeist

I

The Zeitgeist strides upon his way, oblivious to fears,
Down fate's great turnpike thoroughfare that stretches through the years.
Beside this turnpike thoroughfare that stretches through the years

Lived Charles Erastus Gontoseed with numerous compeers.

And Charles Erastus Gontoseed with terror stood aghast,
The Zeitgeist travelled at a gait so reckless and so fast.

So Charles Erastus Gontoseed stood in his onward track
To wrestle with the Zeitgeist and persuade him to hold back.

The Zeitgeist saw not Gontoseed; his look was far away,
But left behind his trampled form mixed with the miry clay.

And then the Zeitgeist still strode on, oblivious to fears,
Down fate's great turnpike thoroughfare that stretches through the years.

II

Beside this turnpike thoroughfare that stretches through the years
Lived William Henry Schlamaheaa with numerous compeers.

And his impulsive temperament chafed in a restive woe,
The Zeitgeist travelled at a gait so lumberly and slow.

So William Henry Schlamahead, the boldest of his race.
Stole in behind the Zeitgeist to accelerate his pace;

Stole in behind the Zeitgeist to accelerate his flight,
And lunged against the Zeitgeist's back and pushed with all his might.

The Zeitgeist travelled on his way, wrapped in eternal peace,
And no one saw his rate of speed perceptibly increase.

But Schlamahead he pushed so hard his nervous system broke.
And he lay stretched a victim to an apoplectic stroke.

And then the Zeitgeist still strode on, oblivious to fears,
Down fate's great turnpike thoroughfare that stretches through the years.

III

And down this turnpike thoroughfare the sons of thunder throng:
The Zeitgeist hears their strife of tongues, and still he strides along.

"Turn to the right," a loud one cries, "and quickly bend about,
For just ahead there stretch afar the bridgeless Bogs of Doubt."

But boldly through the bogs he strides: the mists that wrap the place
Are melted at the coming of the smile upon his face.

"Turn to the left," the voices shout; "the Moonshine Mounts are there.
Transfigured with a lunar grace and rainbow visions fair."

"Turn to the left!" The Zeitgeist still keeps on his endless way;
The Moonshine Mountains have no grace to tempt his feet to stray.

He glances at them with his eye; no more do they exist:
They lift and roll away as fog, and float away in mist.

But still the Zeitgeist travels on, oblivious to fears,
Down fate's great turnpike thoroughfare that stretches through the years.

IV

The Zeitgeist times his marching over mountains and ravines
To the music of an orchestra that plays behind the scenes.

Though we hear not that high, far strain, we march, with all our peers,
To the music of the footfalls of the Zeitgeist through the years.

And the music of those footfalls, though we know not what it means,
Is the music of the orchestra that plays behind the scenes.

So with the Zeitgeist let us march, oblivious to fears,
Down fate's great turnpike thoroughfare that stretches through the years.

The Selectman's Speech

Of elerkunce an' glory all us folks has got our fill,
For we've jest soaked in elerkunce down here in Pokumville.
Las' Thursday wuz the town's birthday — two centuries ol', you see,
An' we had a oratorical an' liter'y jamboree.
Ol' Elder Grimes persided, an' he did the thing up gran',
An' me — I sut beside him, Pokumville's First Sillickman;
Yes, I sut up on the platform there, with all the good an' great,
Sut up there with our Congressman an' Guv'nor of the State.

Our Congressman wuz interduced by Elder Grimes, an' he
Give us an exhibition of his long word filigree;
The Guv'nor, then, he made a speech, a credit to the State,
An' covered us with complimunts an' slung himself first rate.

Then Elder Grimes he riz an' said: "This glorious celebration,
An' this magnificent event, this luminous occasion,

Would be ridikerlous, incomplete, inaderquate an' tame
Without the glorious ornamunt of one illustrous name.

"So I do now persent to you for your supreme ovation
Our most distinguished citerzen, who needs no presentation;
An' I am proud to interduce our foremost citerzen.
The most distinguished Cheerman of our Board of Sillickmen!"

I'd never made a speech afore — I tell ye I wuz scat —
An' I wuz struck so numb an' dumb I didn't know where I 's at;
I gulped an' swallered an' turned red, an' squirmed an' lost my breath,
An' choked an' wiggled an' looked green, an' hankered after death.

An' I stood there for five minutes sure, as I can take my oath;
Stood on my right foot, then my left, then tumbled over both;
An' I'd been glad to welcome death, death or the judgment day —
For I couldn't find to save my life a single word to say.

Bimeby a big gal giggled out, an' this jest made me mad,
An' riled the bottom of my soul an' raised my dander bad.
An' then an' there I jest bust out — an' w'en I once bust out
My words flowed out as smooth an' slick as water from a spout.

I spouted on the grandeur an' the glory of the town,
The splendor of its turnpike road, the beauty of its poun';
The richness of its tater fiel's, whose great crops never fail;
The majesty, magnificence, an' splendor of its jail.

I felt my soul begin to swell, my arms begin to wave.
All life was crammed in that one hour between the cot an' grave;
An' all the elerkunce of time since first the world began
Wuz showered now on Pokumville through her First Sillickman.
An' though I am a bashful stick, jest then I felt sublime
An' loomed before the universe — a figger for all time —
My cuff flew in the organ loft be-end all human reach —
An' I jest deluged Pokumville with cataracts of speech.

My cuff flew off, my collar bust, my whole hair stood up straight;
An' I jest grew from five feet nine right up to ten feet eight.
My arms swished through the air so fast they fairly made it seethe —
The audience wuz still as death, an' no man dared to breathe.

An' still I wouldn't let up a whit — the Guv'nor he turned white
An' run down off the platform steps about half dead with fright.

Our Congressman I hardly saw, he looked so very small —
I walked right over Elder Grimes — didn't notice him at all.

I touched on the new school-house down in Deestrict No. 3.
I gloried in its grandeur, in its grace an' majesty;
I threw my arms from North to South — like flails I let 'em fly —
My feet they shook the centrul earth, my whiskers brushed the sky.

The steeple wabbled on the church an' shook from side to side,
An' Squire Bean's dog give one long howl, fell on his face an' died.
Wen I got through, my clo'es were sp'ilt — an' I was two-thirds dead —
But Pokumville's First Sillickman had made a speech — he had!

The House

When first the builder builds him a house
    'Tis naught but a wooden box, —
A thing of lumber, boards, and planks,
    Of shingles, beams, and blocks;
And when 'tis built 'tis still a box,
    A box to the very minute
Some honest fellow takes the house
    And puts a woman in it.
Then, though it has no gabled front, no turret, tower, or dome,
Then is the builder justified, the box becomes a home.

And why should a man dwell in a house
    Until he lays his head
In the windowless room of the earth-scooped house
    On the hillsides of the dead?
Let him steer the ship by the pilot stars,
    And dig in the sunless mine;
Let him dwell with his flocks on the summer hills,
    And live like a tree or a vine.
The sky is the roof for a brideless man, and the seas are his to roam.
Till he turns to his bride in the builded house, and the box becomes a home.

Why should a man live in a wooden box?
    The ends of the earth are far;
Let him forth to the lands of the Southern Cross
    And the lands of the Polar star.
And meet it is for the brideless man,
    And the dower of his birth,
To draw his strength from the roofless sky

20

And the face of a fenceless earth.
So let him forth till his thoughts shall turn (grown sick with the roofless dome)
To the woman shrined in the builded house, when the box becomes a home.

And when he is sick of the winds of the sky.
    And the old sea's ancient strife,
Let him shear the hills of their pines and build
    A box around his wife.
And then will his chimneyed pine-built box
    Become a templed shrine,
And he'll grow to the virtues that love a roof
    And thrive with the door-yard vine.
And then he shall turn from the unfenced earth, and the sea with its far sky dome,
To the woman shrined in the builded house, when the box becomes a home.

Uncle Hiram's Etiquette

UNCLE HIRAM

I guess I won't run into debt
To buy no book on etikwet;
I ain't much stuck on sich-liku stuff,
Guess I've got etikwet enough.

BOOK AGENT

But here are rules of great variety
On taste, decorum, and propriety;
It gives the highest etiquette
Of fashion's most exclusive set j
It tells us plainly how to act
With grace and elegance and tact
At weddings, feasts, receptions, balls.
And all the fetes in fashion's halls;
How to conduct oneself with grace
At any time, at any place.

UNCLE HIRAM

With them things I hain't no consarn,
For I live mos'ly in my barn;
An' does it tell ye fair an' square
How to conduc' yerself out there?

BOOK AGENT

It tells one how with true propriety
To bear oneself in good society;

21

But in a barn the etiquette
Is hardly that of fashion's set.

UNCLE HIRAM

So fashion has a diffrunt plan?
You know I alius thought a man
Who had a good barn eddication
Was good enough for any station.
I alius keep, I'd have ye larn,
The Ten Comman'ments in my bam.
But I suppose that in society
You've got a new improved variety —
Some rules that you've thought up of late,
For them, I s'pose, are out of date?
Got new comman'ments, I suppose,
That fit men close like tailor's clo'es?
I s'pose the old don't stan' the racket —
Are thrown off like a worn-out jacket?
Old Moscs' rules been out of style
I reckon for consid'ble while?
I keep my barn spruced up an' neat
An' give my cows enough to eat;
An' feed my pigs an' hoss an' mule
An' alius keep the Golden Rule.
But then your book, I calkerlate,
Has got some rules more up to date,
More dickydandified an' smart
That better fit the human heart?
The Golden Rule I s'pose ain't right,
An' you've got suthin' more perlite?
But I'm a poor, ol' duff, you see —
It's good 'nough etikwet for me.

BOOK AGENT

It teaches one good manners and
In language all can understand.

UNCLE HIRAM

As sure as I am Hiram Paul
It don't do no sich thing at all!
Wen you can teach good manners, sir.
Then you can teach a dog to purr,
The sparrer-hawk to dig a hole.
The fox to roost upon a pole.
The elephant to swim the sea,
An' any fish to climb a tree.
Oh, you can make a dummy man

22

Whose clo'es are on the genteel plan
An' dress him in a w'ite cravat.
An' topped off with a stove-pipe hat.
An' part his hair straight down the middle.
An' teach him how his cane to twiddle.
An' how to bow the purtiest way
An' dance an' caper an' sashay —
Sich things are good enough, maybe,
But they ain't manners — no, siree!

BOOK AGENT

Well, sir, if all you've said is true,
What is it you have got to do?

UNCLE HIRAM

You've gotter take a feller's heart
An' scour it in ev'ry part.
An' souse it with the cleansin' soap
Of human helpfulness an' hope.
Rub with a washerwoman's shove
An' soak it in the suds of love;
Then with hot irons you've gotter press
The wrinkled seams er selfishness.
Yes, if a plain ol' duff like me
Has any right to an idee,
I think all manners that don't start
From the deep centre of yer heart
Are merely varnish, on'y fit
For paintin' up a hypocrite.

BOOK AGENT

But don't you think that one should try
To get in good society?

UNCLE HIRAM

Wall, p'raps I may be rather slow,
But I dunno — wall — I dunno —
Can't change yer color, seems to me,
As tree-toads do on ev'ry tree
To jest the color of their perch —
Green on a pine, w'ite on a birch.
A scrub oak in a pasture lot
Don't flourish in a flower pot.
An' it is dangerous to try on
A poodle's collar on a lion.
An' you don't see an eagle stoop
To roost in any chicken coop,
An' you don't see a gosling try
To chase a bob'link through the sky.

An' no socierty I know
In which a feller doesn't grow
As nat'rally as yeller curls
Grow on the heads of baby girls
Can have much comfort for a minute
To the poor rascal that gets in it.
Git in a place where yer didn' grow,
You're like a lily in the snow,
An' yer jest feel as out of place
As whiskers on baby's face.
Oh, you can push by force, I know,
A sliver in a youngster's toe.
An' tain't impossible to pry
A cinder, in a feller's eye:
But when they're there, it's hard to see
How they are pleasant company.
It's hard to teach a poor ol' duff.
Like I be, yer new-fangled stuff;
So I guess I won't run in debt
To buy your book on etikwet.

BOOK AGENT

But surely, sir, you have some friend
To whom the book you'd recommend?

UNCLE HIRAM

You might go in an' see my Sal —
She is my oldest, grown-up gal;
She's sentimental an' is rich
In gush an' potery an' sich;
An' sence she's got that Boston beau
She's full of etikwet and show.
You'd better go an' try her, sir —
You might work off a book on her.

Ownership

I

There is a fiddle I call mine,
   Made of most ancient wood
That in the babyhood of time
   In primal forests stood.
The tree from which my fiddle came
   Grew in a forest glen,
And reached its long arms towards the sky
   Through many lives of men.

But when I try to play a tune
    Upon its ancient strings,
Responsive to my bungling touch,
    Harsh is the song it sings.

There came a beggar to my door
    In raggedness and woe;
He took my fiddle in his hands,
    And drew its ancient bow:
It sang the wind-song of the pine, —
    A voice that weeps and grieves.
Then murmured like the rustling lisp
    Of multitudinous leaves.
And then there came the giant crash
    Of wild wind- driven rain, —
The old tune of the ancient wood
    Played by the hurricane.

And then the sunlight smote the leaves,
    And then there rushed a throng
Of glad bird-voices in a storm
    Of million-throated song.
My fiddle in the beggar's hand
    Sang all the songs it knew
And learned long years ago within
    The wood in which it grew;
And, as I heard those wondrous tunes,
    I could not help but sigh:
"The beggar owns that fiddle of mine;
    He owns it, and not I."

II

Old John McNaughton owns a farm
    Upon the Sandham hills.
Which he, though grumblingly and glum,
    Industriously tills.
He goes to his reluctant toil,
    And labors day by day.
Proclaiming to all men he meets
    That farming does not pay.
But I love John McNaughton's farm,
    I love its hills and dales,
Its orchards vestured in white bloom,
    Its clover-scented vales.

I love the fragrance of its soil.
  Whose incense rises high,
Like whiffs from off an altar stone.
  In worship to the sky.
The brook that through his meadow glides
  Sings to me as it flows
Songs of the hills from whence it came,
  The sea to which it goes.
I lie upon its leafy banks
  In pensive languor curled,
Bosomed in beauty such as graced
  The morning of the world.

I walk upon McNaughton's farm.
  And there this truth descry:
There is no private ownership
  Of earth or air or sky;
And all that's best beneath the stars
  Is mine to have and hold;
The worth that lies beyond all worth
  Cannot be bought and sold.
And, though McNaughton holds his farm
  Heir of an ancient line
And holds the seal-stamped title-deed,
  I know his farm is mine.

The Shaving of Jacob

I've loved that man for forty year,
  I've loved my Jacob dearly;
There ain't no wife in all the worl'
  Loved husband more sincerely;
I've clung to him through good an' bad,
  Through years of work and rest —
An' now he's cut his whiskers off.
  An' looks like all-possesst.
There's nothin' pooty in this worl',
  No really han'some critter,
For Jacob's cut his whiskers off,
  An' life is dark an' bitter.

Them whiskers, once as red as fire,
  Have long been white as snow
An' floated like a snowy flag
  In all the winds that blow;

26

I'd see them whiskers for a mile.
　　An' though I'm growin' blind,
I'd see 'em in the distance an'
　　Knew Jacob was behind.
He'd come home when the sun went down,
　　Come when his work was done,
His whiskers red with sunset an'
　　Far pootier than the sun.

But Jacob when his mind is sot
　　Won't budge for prayers or tears,
An' though I begged him on my knees
　　He slashed 'em with the shears.
The glory has departed now,
　　An' it has broke my heart;
For Jacob's nose an' chin is jest
　　'Bout half an inch apart.
His face looks like our ol' state map
　　Of Massachusetts there;
His chin is jest like ol' Cape Cod
　　A-pintin' in the air.

I've loved that man for forty year
　　An' journeyed by his side.
An' alius, everywhere we went.
　　His whiskers were my pride.
An' now he's cut his whiskers off,
　　All life is stale an' flat.
An' no man's left in all the worl'
　　That's worth a-lookin' at.
I'd like to die — but then I won't — e
　　I want, when I am gone.
No man a-cryin' roun' my grave
　　Without his whiskers on.

Jim and the Universe

Yes, all men knew who talked with him,
The universe was bothering Jim.

He looked through many books to find
For what the cosmos was designed,
How it was made when time begun,
And what 'twas good for when 'twas done.
Through old black-letter scrolls he waded.

27

The schoolmen's folios he invaded,
Through many tomes of thought he went,
To find out what the whole thing meant.
He yearned to find out what it was,
The cause behind the final cause;
He longed to get his fingers on
The *Ding an sich,* the noumenon;
He wished to be equipped to say
What we are here for, anyway.
Just what the cosmos is about,
And learn the things you can't find out.
And all men knew who talked with him,
The universe was bothering Jim.

He read the old Ionian sages,
And spent nine days upon two pages;
And he devoured — a ten years' feast —
The occult wisdom of the East;
He read cuneiform inscriptions,
And hieroglyphs of old Egyptians,
To see if he could find some mention
Of nature's unrevealed intention.
And all men knew who talked with him,
The universe was bothering Jim.
And long and earnest did he pant
Through terminology of Kant,
And with black-livered Schopenhauer
He wept his pessimistic shower.
And modified Pope's hopeful song.
And said, " Whatever is, is wrong."
Through soundless seas of Dutch verbosity,
Through deeps of wide voluminosity.
His onward way grew dark and darker.
Through Schelling, Böhm, and Schleiermacher,
Through Herbart, Hegel, and Jacobi:
No Teuton did he give the "go-by,"
But still the universe was dim.
Opaque and unexplained to Jim.

Of Hobbs and Hume he took his smatter,
And found that there was naught but matter;
And then to Berkeley he inclined,
And found that there was naught but mind j
And then his mental gear grew twisted,
He doubted if himself existed.

And then on Spencer's books he fell
And studied " the unknowable,"
And agonized with many a groan
Because it still remained unknown.
Still all men saw who talked with him,
The universe was bothering Jim.

Weighed down with metaphysic doubt,
Jim in his orchard wandered out;
The blooms had drank the wine of May
And quaffed the freshness of the day;
The fragrance that the west winds blew
Showed the stale earth was good as new;
Beneath a tree down settled Jim,
And let the spring soak into him.

And the glad spring soaked into him,
While pink blooms dropped from every limb;
And then old nature's bookless lore
Did Jim imbibe through every pore,
And wisdom's higher truth did win
By an absorption through his skin.
For he who wants ambrosial fare —
Let him go out and eat the air
When blossom-drunken wild bees boom
Through deeps of perfumed apple-bloom.
There is a dust in library nooks
Blown from the musty leaves of books,
That blinds the lean scholastic's eyes,
And makes him learnedly unwise.
Would you be wise, go out-of-doors,
And just intuit through the pores;
For these white blooms and these blue skies
Were sent to make dull bookmen wise.

So while he drank the vernal day,
Jim lost his cosmical dismay,
Forgot his metaphysic mist,
And felt 'twas glorious to exist;
The sun baked in through Jim's hard skull
A glad sense of the beautiful.
He felt, while apple-blossoms fell,
The universe was fairly well.
And, though it couldn't be understood,
Upon the whole 'twas mainly good.

"I've found, beneath this apple-tree.
The Cosmos is all right," said he.

A Postal-Card Drama

Room No. 5, Academy Hall,
North Cloisterville.

My Dear Friend Paul: —

Have been to school a year to-day,
Crammed Latin, Greek, and algebra;
Although to-day I hardly speak
With fluency in ancient Greek,
Yet Greek next year I hope with ease
To speak like old Demosthenes.
I have one hundred dollars now,
I borrowed of Elias Howe.
    Believe me, yours ever true,

Tom.

July, 1882.

Herdsgrass Four Corners, July 8.

Dear Tom: —
    I write this note to state
That I am on the old farm here,
Where I have puttered round a year.
I've read some fifty new books through —
I borrowed 'em of Elder Drew.
I've bought a horse-rake and a plough,
And got another Jersey cow;
Put fifty dollars in the bank,
And am a slow old farmer crank.
And, now, I guess that this is all,
    From your old Herdsgrass crony,

Paul.

Room No. 5, Academy Hall,
North Cloisterville.

My Old Chum Paul: —
    I've studied Greek another year,
But hardly speak it yet, I fear.
I am, just now, I much regret,
One hundred dollars more in debt.
I borrowed it of Hiram Kent,
And I must pay him eight per cent.
    Now don't neglect to answer me.

Tom.

30

July, 1883.

Herdsgrass Four Corners, July 5.

My Dear Friend Tom: —
   I'm still alive.
Work hard; but John Moore's daughter Pearl
I think a mighty pretty girl.
The days I keep about and stir,
But evenings I read books with her.
Bought two new cows. Have built a shed.
I'm tired — guess I'll go to bed.
Sorry to send you news so small;
They're all I've got.
    Your old friend,

              Paul.

Room No. 5, Academy Hall,
North Cloisterville.

My Dear Old Paul: —

At Greek and Latin still. Regret
I don't know much about 'em yet.
Confounded grind! But Mabel Twing
Is just too sweet for anything!
She is the fairest, purest pearl —
But, Lord! I can't afford a girl.
Borrowed two hundred dollars more.

              Tom.

July, 1884.

Herdsgrass Four Corners, July 9.

Dear Tom: —
   I drop my annual line
To tell you I am farming still.
Bought three new cows of Deacon Hill.
Pearl Moore — my girl — I tell you, sir,
There ain't no other girl like her.
We read together every night.
And through the year we read a sight —
That is — part of the time we read —
The rest we — hem! — Well! I'll proceed;
I've bought a team of Deacon Frank —
Put some more money in the bank.
And pegged on through the year. That's all.
  From your old friend and schoolmate,

              Paul.

31

Dear Old Boy Paul: —

Though I have closed my course at school,
My zeal for knowledge is not cool;
I go to college in the fall —
But Mable Twing — I tell you, Paul,
It does my very nature wring
To separate from Mabel Twing.
We've promised, when I go away
To write each other twice a day.
Have got three hundred dollars now
I borrowed of Erastus Gow.
I hope you flourish still and thrive.

Tom.

July, 1885.

Herdsgrass Four Corners, July 4,

Dear Tom: —

It's time to write once more.
I've settled down, I hope, for Hfe,
And Pearl is just a model wife.
Have been elected Selectman —
Bought three new cows of Neighbor Dan —
Can think of nothing more at all.
From your well-wishing old friend,

Paul.

Grand College, Erudition Hall, July 15.

My Dear Old Paul: —

Have studied like a dog a year,
And life is looking mighty drear;
For Mabel Twing — Oh dear, dear me! —
She's given me the glove, you see.
Borrowed four hundred dollars, too,
Which I must pay when I get through.
I'm in a wretched sort of fix.

Tom.

July, 1886.

Herdsgrass Four Corners, Aug. 8.

Dear Tom: —

I write this postal late,
For young Paul, Jr., came, you see;
Ten pounds; cute rascal! Looks like me.
Elected Selectman again
(Chairman of Board of Selectmen) .
But now I'm tired; it's late at night,

32

And Paul cries so that I can't write.
His lungs are fairly good. That's all.
    From your old friend and schoolmate,

Paul.

Grand College, Erudition Hall, July 14.

My Brave Old Paul: —
    You know that young dude, Percy Prim?
    Well, Mabel Twing has married him.
    Borrowed four hundred dollars more.
    Wish I had angel wings to soar,
    And up to heavenly regions fly.
    Young Percy Prim! I want to die.
    No hope for me this side of heaven.

Tom.

July, 1887.

Herdsgrass Four Corners, July 2.

My Old Friend Tom: —
    There's nothing new.
    Go to the Legislature now,
    And every few days buy a cow.
    Paul, Jr., is a buster. Squall?
    Well, I should say!
                 Your old friend,

Paul.

Grand College, Erudition Hall, July 17.

My Good Old Paul: —
    Greek, Latin, mathematics, stuff!
    The same old grind; got 'bout enough!
    Maude Creighton sets me in a whirl,
    But I shan't try another girl.
    Borrowed five hundred yesterday
    Of our old neighbor, Major Bray.
    My life has grown disconsolate.

Tom.

July, 1888.

Herdsgrass Four Corners, July 9.

Dear Tom: —
    Young Paul is growing fine,
    And now he's most too large to spank;
    I'm cashier of the Herdsgrass Bank,
    Director of the cotton mill,
    Built last July at Bleaker's Hill.

33

But now I hear my youngster call.
And I must stop.

In great haste,

Paul.

My Old Friend Paul: —
    Got through the college; cost like sin;
    And next September I begin
    To study medicine. But, Paul,
    Maude Creighton, she just beats them all!
    She is the angel of my life.
    But, la! I can't support a wife.
    Borrowed five hundred — Maude's divine!

Tom.

July, 1889.

State Senate Chamber, July 3.

Dear Tom: —
    I'm busy as can be.
    I ran against Orlando Bennett
    And now I grace our old State Senate.
    Can stop to write no more at all.
    In breathless haste. Your old friend,

Paul.
Room 40, Esculapian Hall, July 1, '90.

Dear Old Paul: —
    Studying the best that I can do;
    Shall marry Maude when I get through.
  Borrowed more money yesterday
    Of that old skinflint, Major Bray.
    Give love to wife and baby, from
    Your ever new admirer,

Tom.

State Senate Chamber, July 2.

Dear Tom: —
    I've got so much to do
    I'll only send my love, that's all.
    Your ever faithful schoolmate,

Paul.

Room 40, Esculapian Hall, July 15.

My Dear Friend Paul: —
    Maude Creighton's married — wretched flirt!
    To that old soap man, Hiram Burt.
    I'm feeling too "broke up " to cry —

34

All life's a fraud; I want to die.
Receive these broken wailings from
A poor, disconsolate rascal.

Tom.

On Board the Train to Kalamazoo,
Some time in August, '92.

Dear Tom: —

I can't find time to write —
Running for Congress — blamed hard fight.
Will get there if I can — that's all.
So long! Good by!
Your old friend,

Paul.

North Bungtown Turnpike, July 3.

Dear Paul: —

It's time you heard from me.
At last I've hung my shingle out,
And I'm a doctor without doubt;
Have cured two patients of their ills,
But they're too mean to pay their bills.
My creditors throng round like bees —
Send me three thousand dollars, please;
And send it to me without fail
By the next Bungtown Turnpike mail.
Forgive this hasty scribble from
This poor-wretch-on-his-uppers,

Tom.

Congress, Washington, D.C,
September 16, '93.

Dear Tom: —

Your letter just at hand,
Your needs I see and understand.
I know a little clerkship here
That's worth five hundred dolls, per year.
And you can have the place to-day
If you will take it. What d'ye say?
I send you funds to pay your fare.
Brace up, my boy, and don't despair-
I'm sorry that the pay's so small.
But you'll collect it. Yours

Paul.

On Board the Train, Near Shadigee,
September 16, '93.

35

I'm coming fast as steam can race
For that five hundred dollar place.
Accept an ardent blessing from
Your impecunious dead-beat,

Tom.

The Song of the Conquerors

Let us sing the new song of the conquerors of the earth:
    The battle song is still the song that thrills.
Let us sing our song of soldiers, men of wisdom and of worth;
    But the soldier that we sing of never kills.
But he fights with wind and ice-floes in the welter of the seas,
    And he drives his fire-lunged war-horse through the night;
Hear his fire-bowelled courser through the drifted midnight wheeze:
    Here is battle worth the singing! Here is fight!

Let us sing the new song of the conquerors of the world,
    The axemen of the forests of the North;
Their log camp's white smoke-banner on the frozen air unfurled
    Beckons to the waiting millions to come forth.
Old Solitude has nodded on his throne a thousand years,
    But he wakens at the axe stroke. Let him flee:
For he hears the thunder-stallion belching in his tortured ears,
And he hears the roar of cities yet to be.

Let us sing the new song of the conquerors of the earth,
    The song of the ploughmen of the West,
Who make a Land of Plenty where they find a Land of Dearth,
    And lay their hearth-foundations above the adder's nest.
Sing the men who lay the highway where the palace car is whirled,
    And the continent-leaper thunders down the rail;
Strong as men who fought with dragons, tamers of the savage world.
    These are men who fight with Chaos, and prevail.

Let us sing the new song of the conquerors of the earth,
    For the soldier race has not departed yet;
Far up the western mountains see the gunless hosts go forth.
    The soldiers of the Brotherhood of Sweat.
Our war is never ended and the fray is but begun.
    We battle till the coming of the night;
And we'll grapple with our foeman at the setting of the sun;
    We're enlisted while our day lasts. Let us fight!

36

A Cable-Car Preacher

I

"'Tis strange how thoughtless people are"
A man said in a cable-car,
" How careless and how thoughtless," said
The Loud Man in the cable-car.
And then the Man with One Lame Leg
Said softly, "Pardon me, I beg.
For your valise is on my knee;
It's sore," said he of One Lame Leg.

II

A woman then came in with twins
And stumbled o'er the Loud Man's shins;
And she was tired half to death,
This Woman Who Came in with Twins.
And then the Man with One Lame Leg
Said, " Madam, take my seat, I beg."
She sat, with her vociferant twins.
And thanked the Man of One Lame Leg.

III

" 'Tis strange how selfish people are,
They carry boorishness so far;
How selfish, careless, thoughtless," said
The Loud Man of the cable-car.
A Man then with the Lung Complaint
Grew dizzy and began to faint;
He reeled and swayed from side to side,
This poor Man with the Lung Complaint.

IV

The Woman Who Came in with Twins
Said, " You can hardly keep your pins;
Pray, take my seat." He sat, and thanked
The Woman Who Came in with Twins.
The Loud Man once again began
To curse the selfishness of man;
Our lack of manners he bewailed
With vigor, did this Loud, Loud Man.

But still the Loud Man kept his seat;
　　A Blind Man stumbled o'er his feet;
The Loud Man preached on selfishness,
　　And preached, and preached, and kept his seat
　　The poor Man with the Lung Complaint
　　Stood up — a brave, heroic saint —
And to the Blind Man, " Take my seat,"
　　Said he who had the Lung Complaint.

VI

The Loud Man preached on selfish sins;
　　The Woman Who Came in with Twins,
The poor Man with the Lung Complaint,
　　Stood, while he preached on selfish sins.
　　And still the Man with One Lame Leg
　　Stood there on his imperfect peg
And heard the screed on selfish sins —
　　This patient Man with One Lame Leg.

VII

The Loud Man of the cable-car
　　Sat still and preached and travelled far.
The Blind Man spake no word unto
　　The Loud Man of the cable-car.
　　The Lame-Legged Man looked reconciled,
　　And She with Twins her grief beguiled.
The poor Man with the Lung Complaint —
　　All stood, and sweetly, sadly smiled.

The News

I'm a reporter out for news,
　　And by this woodland fountain, .
I am commissioned by my chief
　　To interview this mountain.
Ah, me! but I've a nose for news,
　　A nose of some refinement;
And so I gladly thank my chief
　　And take up my assignment.

There's nothing happens in the crowd;
    I leave the newsless town;
There's news out here upon the hills
    That's well worth writing down.
"So now, my Mountain, what's the news?
    What tidings from afar?
For you have gossiped with the winds
    And talked with every star.

"Now let me hear the best or worst
    And take the news to town;
I'm here with pencil and with pad
    To take the message down."
"Ah, zealous scribe," the Mountain saith,
    "But I have news to tell;
Take down and publish wide and far,
    'The Universe is well.'

"I reach down to the central fires,
    And upward to the sky;
And none for all the news that's going
    Has better chance than I.
I've learned while standing high and deep.
    And looking far around,
That health is at the core of things,
    The heart of life is sound.

"Heed not the weak wail of the town
    About the world's despair,
But know the uncontaminate hills
    Are virginal and fair.
The race of man, they say, grows old
    And wanders from the truth;
Let them go forth upon the hills
    And share the mountains' youth.

"The winds are strong, the storms are loud,
    But I stand firm enough;
The bases of the world are laid
    On very solid stuff.
The Winds that from the salt seas blow,
    They tell me, listening dumb,
The sea can keep the old earth fresh
    Some million years to come.

"No suns have clashed, no planets burst.
    The worlds whirl on their way;
The day makes beautiful the night,
    The night makes glad the day.
I listen to the stars afar.
    And to the mountains near;
But all the news that comes my way
    Is news I'm glad to hear.

"So, zealous scribe, take down my news,
    'Tis good enough to tell.
Take down and publish wide and far,
    "The Universe is well.'"
Good news, all this, from one who knows;
    And now, at set of sun,
I take my pad and journey home —
    A good day's work is done.

The Little Red Stamp

I'm the little red stamp with George Washington's picture;
    I have the right of way:
And the mail train thunders from under the stars
    And rattles into the day.
Now clear the rail for your Uncle Sam's mail;
    Ye freight trains, stand aside!
Spur your iron-lunged horse to his fullest speed
    For the little red stamp would ride.
So vomit your flame on the startled night
    And your smoke in the face of the day:
For the little red stamp with George Washington's picture
    Must have the right of way.

The engine ploughs, when I start on my ride,
    Through the drifted banks of snow;
But we hasten to climes where the rivers melt
    And climes where the roses blow.
First the pines of Maine, then the Kansan plain,
    Then whiffs from the Western Bay.
Till I drop in the hands that have reached for me
    A thousand leagues away.
Pull open the throttle and loose every brake,
    And dash through the night and the day;

For the little red stamp with George Washington's picture
   Must have the right of way.

I'm the little red stamp with George Washington's picture.
   And I go wherever I may,
To any spot in George Washington's land;
   And I go by the shortest way.
And the guns of wrath would clear my path,
   A thousand guns at need,
Of the hands that should dare to block my course
   Or slacken my onward speed.
Stand back! Hands off of Uncle Sam's mail!
   Stand back there! Back! I say;
For the little red stamp with George Washington's picture
   Must have the right of way.

The Prayer of Cyrus Brown

"The proper way for a man to pray,"
Said Deacon Lemuel Keyes,
"And the only proper attitude
Is down upon his knees."

"No, I should say the way to pray,"
Said Rev. Dr. Wise,
Is standing straight with outstretched arms
And rapt and upturned eyes."

"Oh, no; no, no," said Elder Slow,
"Such posture is too proud:
A man should pray with eyes fast closed
And head contritely bowed."

"It seems to me his hands should be
Austerely clasped in front.
With both thumbs pointing toward the ground,"
Said Rev. Dr. Blunt.

"Las' year I fell in Hodgkin's well
Head first," said Cyrus Brown,
"With both my heels a-stickin' up,
My head a-pinting down;

"An' I made a prayer right then an' there —
Best prayer I ever said,

41

The prayingest prayer I ever prayed,
A-standing on my head."

The World-Reformer and His Wife

Said Farmer John to Joiner Ned:
"Come put a back door on my shed."

Says Joiner Ned to Farmer John:
"I cannot put your back door on.
The Guild I'm interested in
For the abolishment of sin,
Meets at my house this very day,
And so I cannot get away."

"Well, after you've abolished sin
Come down to-morrow and begin;
I want that back door on my shed,"
Said Farmer John to Joiner Ned.

"To-morrow, neither, can I come,
The Friends of the Millennium
Meet at the house of Deacon Kent,
And I am first Vice-President."

"Well, then, next Wednesday, without doubt.
When your millennium's started out.
Just let it take its course and spread,
And put that back door on my shed."

"I read an essay Wednesday, John,
Before the Culture Club, upon
'The Easiest Method to Restore
Our Long- Lost Eden Here Once More;'
To foster peace, abolish war,
And render virtue popular."

"Well, get your Eden here all right
By sundown, prompt, next Wednesday night;
And then, next Thursday morning, Ned,
Come put that back door on my shed."

"The Anti-Hunger Club convenes
Next Thursday, down to Hiram Green's.

And I have promised to orate
On how to crush and extirpate
Man's tendency for fish and meat.
His grovelling desire to eat."

"But won't you come down, by and by.
We'll say two years from next July?
You'll have your various schemes put through.
You'll have the universe built new;
Come down, then, with your tool-kit, Ned.
And put that back door on my shed."

"I think," says Ned, " I'll take that chance
If you will pay me in advance;
For my wife says that we've no meat
Or flour in the house to eat:
This cash may save domestic strife
And kind of pacify my wife."

Sempronius Fitz

Sempronius Fitz
Lived by his wits
And spurned the thought of labor.
"Why toil for bread
And clothes?" he said,
"While I can sponge my neighbor?"
His dainty feet were never set
Among the swinking sons of sweat.

"The greatest ban
That's known to man
Is industry," he muttered.
"I'll find, I say.
Some other way
To get my biscuit buttered;
I'll find some other way," he said,
"To oleomargarine my bread."

With purpose big
To shun fatigue
And toil's severe coercion,
He wouldn't exert
Himself to hurt

43

Except to shun exertion.
All other work he'd always shirk
Except the task of shunning work.

Sempronius Fitz
Lived by his wits
And did no formal labor,
And made a good.
Fair livelihood
By sponging from his neighbor.
But, though his whole aim was to shirk,
He died at last of overwork.

Worked like a Turk
To keep from work
Did our good friend Sempronius.
But several score
Of thousands more
Hold this same creed erroneous:
That any man can sponge his neighbor
And live a life devoid of labor.

But by a great
Sarcasm of Fate,
Who never sanctions shirking.
These Sons of Rest
The oftenest
Are killed by overworking.
So fast from labor's pains they fly
That the exertion makes them die.

Uncle Seth on the Modern Novel

Them novelists who write to-day, w'y, they hain't got the trade.
There ain't a one that knows jest how a story should be made;
Not one who understands the thing, not one who does the job,
An' not a one who slings himself like ol' Sylvanus Cobb.
Ah, ol' Sylvanus Cobb, my boy, w'en he was on the deck,
We had a story-teller then of giant intelleck.

The hero of a story now he don't git in no row:
No Injuns, an' no piruts, an' no villains, anyhow.
The hero of to-day is tame; hain't got no whiz an' whirl;
Sets still an' lets some other chap go in an' court his girl!
The novelists who write to-day have all mistook their job;

Not one has got the glor'us gift of ol' Sylvanus Cobb.

Sylvanus took *his* hero where a hero ought to go,
In scrapes an' awful dangers where he seemed to have no show;
He drowned him, shot him, scalped him, but every reader knew
Sylvanus knew his business well and he would pull him through.
He bruised him, banged him, buried him, an' did a han'some job.
But still we knew the chap was safe with ol' Sylvanus Cobb.

He'd git the chap in dungeons deep, with soldiers all about,
To fill his body full of shot if he should once git out;
Sylvanus was too shrewd for that, an' alius had in stock
A subterranus passageway through which the chap could walk.
An' though he slashed an' slaughtered him, he understood his job;
We knowed that we could trust the man with ol' Sylvanus Cobb.

We'd see the hero's funeral, we'd hear the parson pray,
We'd see his coffin in the tomb, all neatly packed away.
But that didn't worry us a bit. Above the yawnin' grave
We knowed Sylvanus still was there, an' he had power to save.
We'd leave him in the grave content, an' we didn' care a pin.
We knowed Sylvanus knowed the trick to git him out ag'in.

While Sylvanus led his hero we were not a bit afraid,
Though he marched ag'in an army an' he faced a cannonade;
Though a mine should cave in on him, though a whirlpool sucked him in,
We all trusted to Sylvanus to produce him sound ag'in.
An' Sylvanus alius done it. Oh, he understood the job;
We knowed that we could trust the man with ol' Sylvanus Cobb.

Give me them good ol' days of guns, of snakes, an' gapin' jaws,
Of wolves an' ragin' catamounts, with blood upon their paws;
W'en six-foot heroes courted girls that they had snatched away
From out a bloody bandit's clasp, an' tramped him into clay.
I wish we had some writers now who understood the job,
Some writers who could sling themselves like ol' Sylvanus Cobb!

Miss Sophronia's Tragic Cure

He treated me for mumps, did the blessed Dr. Stumps,
He treated me for measles when my soul was in the dumps;
And without a shade of question he improved my indigestion —
Oh! a therapeutic wonder was the blessed Dr. Stumps!

But when my mumps had fled then I had an aching head,

And when my head was cured I had lung-complaint, instead;
Then he clinched with my bronchitis, then he treated my gastritis —
And now that blessed doctor — he has left me — he is dead!

When he used to come and say, "Ah! you have the chills to-day!"
Or, "You have a touch of fever," I was frolicsome and gay;
When he told me, "Miss Sophronia, you are suffering with pneumonia,"
I rejoiced with great rejoicing at the words he used to say.

For he'd sit and sympathize with compassion in his eyes,
And he talked about my symptoms and he'd look superbly wise;
Then he'd give me learned theses on the treatment of diseases,
And number all the catalogue of all my agonies.

While the long years rolled away I was very sick and gay,
I was very ill and happy, gladly wasting in decay;
But when Dr. Stumps departed. Dr. Myers, iron-hearted.
Came and cured me in a fortnight — and I'm sad and well to-day.
Now I have no blessed ease that accompanies disease —
What is there in life to cheer me? What is there in life to please?
Now I have no blessed theses on my symptoms and diseases —
If I must continue healthy let me die and find release.

To See the Thing Go On

"What's all this thing about? " says he.
    "Wall, I dunno," says I.
"What good is all this worl' to me,
    This lan' an' sea an' sky?
The same ol' thing! Git up an' dress,
    An' eat an' work like sin;
Then go to bed, git up an' dress,
    An' eat an' work ag'in.
What's all this thing about? " says he.
    Says I: " Can't tell ye, John;
But, as for me, I like to see,
    To see the thing go on.

"There ain't no end to this machine.
    An' no man hereabout,
So fur as I have ever seen.
    Can tell what it grinds out;
Its belts are hitched to far-off gears.
    Far out be-end the sun,

An' I've no doubt 'twill run for years
    The way it alius run."
"But what's the thing about?" says he:
    Says I, " Can't tell ye, John;
But, as for me, I like to see.
    To see the thing go on."

"'Tis day an' night an' night an' day,
    The same ol' thing," says John.
" I guess it is," says I, " but say.
    Let's watch the thing go on;
For all the grass an' things that grow,
    An' stars, it seems to me,
Are jest a free-for-nothin' show,
    For us deadheads to see.
An' I ain't tired of it yit.
    It's pretty middlin', John:
An', as for me, I like to see.
    To see the thing go on.
"I like to see the thing, my friend,
    'Tis healthy sport for man.
Though I can't tell ye where 'twill end.
    Nor where the thing began."
"What's all the thing about? " " Dunno
    'Tis fun enough for me
To jest lay back an' see the show
    An' wonder; yes, sir-ee!
An' so I guess that we are here,
    An' that's our business, John.
To work an' git ourselves in gear
    To help the thing go on."

An Honest Man

I hed a cow w'en I set out to bull' my fortune up,
One hoe, one shovel, an' one spade, an' one good brindle pup.
But my stout heart an' my soun' hed an' these two han's, you see.
An' my unekalled honesty hez brung me where I be.

This is the lesson I impress on ev'ry noble youth,
Integrerty, moralerty, an' honesty, an' trooth.
Integrerty, moralerty, an' honesty, you see.
With my good heart an' hed an' han' hez brung me where I be.

Merried the daughter of the man where I wuz hired man.
An' w'en he died we got his farm — he willed it all to Nan.
I hired good town paupers then to do my work for me,
For they'll eat feed that common men won't look at, don't yer see?

So I saved money this way — I saved, but never spent —
An' I loaned it to my neighbors, an' they gave me ten per cent.
I loved my neighbors like myself, rich, poor, an' great an' small.
An' put a morgidge on their farms to 'commodate 'em all.

An' Widow Barclay, reckless soul, spent all her husban' left.
Just bringin' up her children — W'y, it seems almost like theft;
" W'y, sich extravagance as that," sez I, " will never do."
An' I foreclosed her morgidge, for it was my duty to.

An' neighbor Bunker's wife wuz sick; he spent his cash fer pills.
Jest squandered all his earnin's on them worthless doctors' bills;
I couldn' approve his reckless way, an' as a repermand,
I jest foreclosed his morgidge an' then annexed his land.
An' ol' man Babson, down the crick, wuz gettin' lame and blind,
His farm wuz growin' up 'ith weeds, his hayin' wuz behind:
Sez I, " 'Tis time this good ol' man wuz laid upon the shelf" —
So I foreclosed his morgidge an' I took his farm myself.

So, I've been a morril power, an' through all the neighborhood,
I've gone about, like men of ol', engaged in doin' good;
An' I hev foun' that goodness pays, an' vircher is divine.
For all my reckless neighbors' farms hev all been jined to mine.

This is the lesson I impress on ev'ry noble youth,
Integrerty, moralerty, an' honesty, an' trooth.
Integrerty, moralerty, an' honesty, you see,
With my good heart, an' hed an' han' hez brung me where I be.

A Good Domestic Man

Ah, once I dreamed the fane of fame,
    Whose turrets rise and soar,
I'd enter with a loud acclaim.
    Stride through its open door;
I'd tread its loud-resounding halls
And hang my portrait on its walls,
    And lead the vanguard's van:
But now I have one only hope,
To live within my modest scope,

48

A good domestic man;
To live in gentle peace serene,
A quiet fixture in the scene,
   A good domestic man.

And once I dreamed the sage's lot
   My studious days should charm,
To sit on beetling heights of thought
   In philosophic calm;
I thought to sit and lucubrate
On time and space, on force and fate.
   And sift thought's wheat from bran;
But half a dozen girls and boys
Disturb the sage-like equipoise
   Of a domestic man.
A pandemonium of sound
Does not conduce to thought profound
   In a domestic man.
To walk with sons of Poesy
   I made my youthful vow,
A fiery frenzy in mine eye,
   A laurel on my brow:
A mighty vista, long and lone,
Stretched to an intellectual throne,
   And toward the throne I ran:
But I gave up that goal to be
A model domesticity,
   A good domestic man.
Who cares for thrones his thoughts to rouse,
Who has a baby in the house?
   No good domestic man.

And once I dreamed to march to fame
   Through seas of bloody slaughter.
And make our rivers flowing tame
   Run fierce with blood, not water.
But now I've learned to understand
How to obey, but not command.
   To heed my general's plan;
And, with no rude rebellious sin,
Revolt against my discipline —
   A good domestic man.
And when my young twins disagree.
Why, then there's war enough for me,
   A good domestic man.

O'Flaherty and Stubbs

A man of wondhrous clarity
Of uttherance wuz O'Flaherty.
He sid jist phwat he hid to say
   Wid ghreat oraculahrity:
   It might nat be ghrammatical.
   But, gor! it was emphatical.
Fer he was always did cock-shure
   Decided an' daghmatical;
   An' very fool of spache
      He wuz;
   Of t'oughts beyand our rache
      He wuz.
   He talked wid ghreat velarcity,
   Wus fool of ghreat pamparsity,
   Of langwidge an' verbarsity,
      He wuz,
      Indade!

There wuz no shimularity
Bechune Stubbs an' O'Flaherty.
O'Flaherty wuz fool of worruds;
   But Stubbs he shpake wid rahrity.
   John Stubbs bed no saghacity
   In spache an' no loquahcity;
For worruds an' phrazeology
   John Stubbs hid no capahcity.
   A still, doomb sart of choomp
      He wuz,
   A quiet sart of goomp
      He wuz;
   But Stubbs he loved O'Flaherty
   Wid love of wondhrous rahrity
   Wid most sthupendous charity,
      He did,
      Yis, sor!

An' I must shtate O'Flaherty
He chirished t'oughts of charity
For Stubbs, although bechune the two
   There was a ghreat dispahrity;
   No incomphatability
   Could ginerate harstility;

Bechune O'Flaherty an' Stubbs
   There reigned a great thranquillity.
   Their love it wuz so great
         They wuddent.
   They could not, separhate;
         They cuddent.
   Through great disshimularity
   Did Stubbs an' did O'Flaherty
   Keep mootchul parpulahrity;
         They did,
         Gor, yis!

   For Stubbs unarstentatiously
   Wud sit and dhrink voraciously;
O'Flaherty's verbarsity
   He poured out so loquaciously,
   His spache he wud not spam it, he
   Wud sit in tacitarnity;
Yis, while O'Flaherty hild forth.
   He'd sit to all etarnity;
   And so while one sit still.
         He did,
   The other shpake his fill.
         He did;
   An thus growed up afifiction mellow
   Bechune this doomb an' talkin' fellow,
   Bechune this goomp and tongue propeller,
         There did —
         That's all!

Melchizedek Jones's Modern Thanksgiving

Melchizedek Adoniram Jones, two hundred years ago,
In peaceful rest laid down his bones and left this world of woe;
A Puritan of ancient breed, sweet may his soul repose;
A man who loved his holy creed and preached it through his nose.

The spirit of Melchizedek Jones roamed through the fields of light.
Walked o'er the City's golden stones by rivers of delight;
But once upon Thanksgiving day he heard a sound of mirth
Come floating heavenward on its way from the rejoicing earth.

"Ah, me," says he, "this is the day we 'stablished long ago;
How quick the years have rolled away, how fast the centuries go.

I fain once more would see the earth, though after many years,
From which this most unseemly mirth is floating to my ears."

Melchizedek Adoniram Jones then slipped away to earth
And sought the town where rest his bones, the town that gave him birth.
His great-great-great-great grandson's home he entered boldly free,
And said, " I will no longer roam; here I abide with thee."

"But why, my great-great-great," said he, "why this ungodly glee?
Why this unhallowed revelry, this graceless jollity?
Turn ye from wanton pleasure's path, refrain from this mad mirth,
Lest I arise and in my wrath I smite ye to the earth.

"What vain apparel I behold, thine helpmeet's proud array —
The silks of Sidon and the gold of Tarshish shall decay.
Thy gold shall tarnish, jewels rust, and fade thy silken sashes —
Away and sit thee in the dust in sackcloth and in ashes.

"Out with your tinkling music vain, your loud abomination;
More fitting were a funeral strain to mourn your desolation;
The furnace of my wrath is hot, my righteous anger high,
I'll cry aloud and spare ye not, and smite ye hip and thigh.

"And these vain books, the vainest thing the heart of man entices,
So full of vain imagining and many strange devices —
And Shakespeare too? Still 'neath the stars lives his unhallowed mirth?
I trusted our anathemas had driven him from earth.

"Why gorge ye with this foolish spoil and make a feasting day.
This wealth of meat and wine and oil, when ye should fast and pray?
And wherefore is this riotous feast, these Egypt fleshpots here?
Why gorge ye like the gluttonous beast, when ye should quake with fear?

"Why make your children such a din, why is their glee so great?
Depraved — conceived and born in sin and wholly reprobate —
Before their great sins let them quail, and let their grief be deep;
In contrite sorrow let them wail and gnash their teeth and weep."

"Good saint," replied his great-great-great, "I note your warm appeal,
Your manners may not be ornate though I respect your zeal;
But we believe that childish pranks spring not from Satan's guile,
And men may Oner heartfelt thanks and keep their clothes in style.

"But come, my great-great-great, sit down and try our modern fare;

Relax your Puritanic frown and smooth your ruffled hair."
The Puritan began to eat, his frown it passed away;
He felt the kindly influence sweet — the spirit of the day.

The turkey vanished like a dream, the pudding did not stay,
The viands in a steady stream all seemed to flow his way;
And him-ward, all that dinner hour, the stream of victuals poured,
And his assimilative power astonished all the board.

Between the pudding and the pie he lifted up his voice,
"Rejoice! rejoice!" they heard him cry, "again I say rejoice!
Give thanks for this your modern lot, and all your modern bliss.
I wish," he said, "John Endicott could taste a meal like this!"

A Consolidated Ghost

On July Fifth at Charon's ferry,
    Near Peter's gate,
Two spirits meet. Note closely very
    The place and date.

'Twas July Fifth, as I have stated.
    These spirits met;
On July Fourth they'd celebrated —
    Ah, vain regret!

By that lone shore at Charon's ferry
    These spirits meet;
And they are somewhat fragmentary
    And incomplete.

One spirit by the other hngers
    Like ghosts bereft;
Says One to Two, "How many fingers
    Have you still left?"

"I have three fingers," says the other;
    "And what have you?"
"Alas! " he says, "my friend and brother,
    I have but two."

"How many ribs are still remaining
    Intact to you?"
"I have four ribs — I ain't complaining,"

53

Says Number Two.

"I have one ear, one eye, a fraction
    Of one backbone,
A partial nose unfit for action,"
    Says Number One.

"I have three teeth, one lung, one shoulder.
    One eye, like you,
One leg — but one's enough to hold yer."
    Says Number Two.

"Let us two coalesce and mingle,"
    Said One to Two:
"We are too fragmentary single.
    Now what say you?"

Says Two to One, "With acclamation
    I hail your plan;
For two of us in combination
    Will make one man."

And so to make themselves completer
    They rolled in one;
And looking on did good St. Peter
    Exclaim, "Well done!

"Now enter in, henceforth inherit
    Rest without sin."
Then the consolidated spirit
    Did enter in.

The Unexpressed

I

Once there was a poor old hack
    Who had to write for bread,
Who meant to write an epic poem
If any time his wife should show him
    They'd bread enough ahead;
But need kept pace with the supply
Until his time had come to die.

Once there was a music-seer
    Who heard strange anthems roll.

Eternal melodies from far,
Like voices from an unseen star,
    Beat in upon his soul.
But he to earn the rabble's praise
Played rub-a-dub music all his days.

A dreaming builder once there was
    Who dreamed of tower and dome;
Who dreamed of great cathedral piles,
Of sounding naves and pillared aisles
    To shame the pomp of Rome;
But he with untoward fate at strife.
Built wooden houses all his life

II

This poet's soul went out at night
    And up the Path of Souls;
And Homer met him at the gate
And welcomed him as if a mate
    Upon the eternal rolls.
"Souls know," he said, " the songs unsung
As well as those that find a tongue."

This dead musician's soul went forth
    Into the darkness drear —
A glad voice smote the clouds apart —
The brother-greeting of Mozart,
    Who hailed him as his peer.
"Souls know," he said, " that music best
That haunts the dumb soul unexpressed."

This builder's lone soul took its flight
    Weighed down with mighty woe;
But felt its lifted wings expand
To see the beckoning of the hand
    Of Michael Angelo.
"Your unbuilt domes," exclaimed the shade,
"Shame all the domes I ever made."

Keep on Just the Same

Young Peter, when he "spoke his piece"
    Before the school committee,
The superintendent, and a crowd
    From all parts of the city,

Trembled and shook in every limb,
    His heart beat like a flail.
His face alternate blazed with fire
    Or turned a deadly pale;
But Peter was of hero stuff,
    A raw recruit of fame;
Though he was frightened half to death,
    He kept on just the same.

In after years, when he proposed
    To Miss Ophelia Gleason,
His trepidation was intense
    Beyond all rule or reason:
He choked and stammered, hemmed and hawed,
    And blushed a rosy red;
It was so hard to be alive
    He wished that he was dead.
But, like the brave young man he was,
    He made her change her name:
Though he was frightened half to death
    He kept on just the same.

Fate loves the fellow who is scared,
    Who trembles in his dread,
But when his fears cry out, "Don't go I"
    His will cries, "Go ahead!"
So Peter chmbed his fears like stairs,
    And every fear subdued
But raised him to a higher plane
    And sunnier altitude.
He left his youth's obscurer mists,
    And climbed the crags of fame;
Though he was frightened half to death,
    He kept on just the same.

There is a slave whose name is Fear,
    A trembling, cringing thing;
There is a king whose name is Will,
    And every inch a king.
The king and slave have their abodes.
    And work their joint control.
Their mingled work of blight and bloom.
    In every mortal's soul.
But strong is he who heeds the king,

And laughs the slave to shame;
Who, although frightened half to death,
   Still keeps on just the same.

Go, fight the battles of the day,
   The spectres of the night,
And, though you tremble with your fears,
   Still tremble on — and fight.
What though the man turn pale with fear,
   And quake and tremble long,
If the proud will within the man
   Be resolute and strong?
Then throne king Will within the man,
   And laugh slave Fear to shame;
Though you are frightened half to death,
   Still keep on just the same.

Chet Colder and His Whale

Chet Golder told to every man
   The strange, miraculous tale,
How he one time, off Yucatan,
   Was swallowed by a whale.
"Our ship," said Chet, "was in a gale,
   An' sich a wind wuz blown
I, in the wide mouth of a whale.
   Plumb off the deck was thrown.
But the terbacker which I chew,
   The whale gave sich a pain.
That on the deck from which I blew
   He threw me up again."

For forty years did Chet maintain
   This story strange and grim,
Until young Lawyer Simon Lane
   Applied the screws to him.
"Now, Uncle Chet," young Lane said he,
   "How long in that whale's power,
In his interior might you be?"
   Chet answered, "Half an hour."
"And did the whale then swim away?"
   Chet answered, "He stood still."
"The wind was blowing then, you say?"
   Chet answered, "Fit to kill."

"And so your ship stood motionless
    In that wild hurricane,
Until the whale in his distress
    Should throw you up again?"
"Why, no, yer big fool," answered Chet,
    "In sich a fearful blow
A ship would drift as you can bet,
    A dozen miles or so."
"So when the whale your form upthrew
    On that eventful day.
He aimed and hit the ship with you
    Some dozen miles away?"
"Wall, how so fur I could be thrown,"
    Chet said, "I hardly see
And can't explain, as I'll be blown.
    How sich a thing could be."
"Now, Uncle Chet, just look at me
    And answer plain and slow;
"Now — did you — ever — go to sea?"
    And Chet he answered, "No!"
"But how about this life-long tale
    You've told to every man,
Of deglutition by a whale
    Down there off Yucatan?"

Then Chet he scratched and scratched his head,
    And slow he made reply,
And with a puzzled look he said:
    "It must have been a lie.
But it hez been a comfort. Si,
    I've told it from my youth.
Until I thought, myself, this lie
    Wuz nothin' but the truth.
This unbelievin' age, yer see,
    So loves to poke an' pry,
'Twon't let a poor ol' man like me
    Believe in his own lie."

O'Meara's Cosmic Pioneer

Born to re-animate his era
Was young Erastus Jones O'Meara;
For this young hero of my verse
Was born to search the universe,

To sail through the unbounded skies
And all the cosmos scrutinize;
To sail through cosmos to the reign
Of chaos, and sail back again.

It was his cherished hope to rise
A great Columbus of the skies,
To sail through ether's star-isled seas
As sailed the mighty Genoese,
And earn a name beyond compare
As the great admiral of the air.
He hoped to float off on the breeze
Through those unsailed aerial seas.
And find new Indies and new races
Out in the interstellar spaces.

As old times gave Magellan birth
To circle the ungirdled earth.
So had this late transcendent era
Brought forth Erastus Jones O'Meara,
The hero of this halting verse,
To girdle the wide universe;
And 'twas the end of his emprise
The cosmos to Magellanize.

Before he launched forth all alone
Into the limitless unknown,
'Twas indispensable, I ween,
To make a first-class flying- machine.
And he's the greatest of his race.
    The climax of consummate brain,
Who'll build a ship to sail through space
    And then sail back again.
But this Erastus Jones O'Meara,
The topmost flowerage of his era, —
This feat, from all past ages hid,
Erastus Jones O'Meara did.

And so he made a flying- machine,
The best the world had ever seen:
Its levers worked with perfect ease,
Its pistons did not grind or wheeze,
Its belts all moved without constriction.
Its cog-wheels whirled and made no friction.
Its broad wings flapped with graceful swing

When young Erastus pulled the string;
They moved with grace so grand and regal
That they improved upon the eagle.
"When it gets in the air up yonder,"
Erastus said, "'twill beat the condor,
And sail as grandly through the skies
As any bird of paradise;
Yes, sail the seas of space across,
An interstellar albatross! "
And then he painted large and clear
In words that he considered terse,
"O'Meara's Cosmic Pioneer
    and Searcher of the Universe."

So, when this great machine was done,
'Twas made to sail beyond the sun.
Between all parts of this creation
There was a mutual adaptation,
A harmony of part and whole
That made it like a living soul:

Perfect in piston, belt, and line,
A unity of grand design.
No blemish had this flying-machine.
No fault that any man could spy.
Except this single fault, I ween, —
No living man could make it fly.

"But that's all right," he said. " You'll own
No flying-machine has ever flown;
And my machine has stood the test
And turned out good as all the rest.
A man's abilities are high
Who'll cause a flying-machine to fly.
And mine will do it, I declare,
When I have fixed that pedal there.
And filed that cog-wheel down a mite,
And screwed that middle screw in tight;
And early next week I shall fly.
Start in and navigate the sky."

He fixed his pedal, screwed his screw,
His cog-wheel filed, and tried anew;
The wings they flapped with perfect poise.
And worked without superfluous noise.

60

They bravely reached up toward the sky,
And looked as if they ought to fly;
They looked as if they ought to climb
The great translunar heights sublime,
And make a wide extended flight
Out into " chaos and old night."
But truth the poet must revere.
    And I must brutally assert,
"O'Meara's Cosmic Pioneer"
    Stayed stationary in the dirt;
Still in the dust and dirt it stayed
In the old wood-shed where 'twas made.
O'Meara worked from day to day
Till his brown hair had turned to gray;
And with life's leaf no longer green
He tinkered on his old machine;
Impelled by his undying hope,
He fixed a cord or trained a rope,
Or loosed a belt, or shaved a beam,
And lived his life and dreamed his dream;
And then he died, as all men die;
That's all — he never learned to fly.
That's all? Ah, no! for all life's scenes,
Filled with unflying flying-machines.
Attest that all men everywhere
Are navigators of the air;
We all make fair machines to rise
To sunset islands of the skies,
Through oceans without rocks or bars.
Whose archipelagoes are stars;
And all good men until they die
Make flying- machines that will not fly.

And shall our flower of hope contract
And freeze in these cold winds of fact:
That the round sky is very high.
And flying-machines can never fly?
No, woe to him who has no gleam
From the bright starlight of a dream,
Who never sees the stars draw nigh,
And never dreams that he can fly!
So hammer on in hope serene,
    And never falter till you die;
Some day there'll be a flying-machine
    That in reality will fly.

Suspender Souls

He sold suspenders at the fair,
    And loud he shouted, loud and well,
That none might pass him unaware
    That he had "galluses" to sell.
If would-be purchasers were coy,
    'Twas thus his loud oration ran:
" They're short enough for any boy,
And long enough for any man."
And thus we saw this vender's "brace"
Was suited to the human race.

Send us strong souls that find it joy
    To live on this "suspender" plan;
Souls meek enough for any boy.
    And proud enough for any man;
Souls that can stand up unafraid.
    Erect before the highest throne,
And own the lowest soul that's made
    A twin-born brother of their own.
Send this " suspender " type of men
Through every mart and field and glen.
Send souls on this " suspender " plan
    Whose "stretch" no caste can e'er destroy:
Souls that stretch up to any man,
    Souls that reach down to any boy;
Souls that can say, " I'm good as you,
    I'm good as you, however high;
And you, and you, however low.
    However low, are good as I," —
Souls that both high and low can own
As twin-born brothers of their own.

The Twilight of The Poets

Away down in Asia Minor there, when Homer sang his song,
His poetry, the critics said, was very far from strong;
And while he twanged his lyre there, this blind old singing Greek,
The critics called attention to its inartistic squeak.
So then and there the story of Achilles' wrath fell flat,
And scarce a coin was dropped within the blind old beggar's hat.
"There once were geniuses," they said, "who thronged the world about.
They once were numerous as grass; but now we are just out."

Of course, the world was very old and song had lost its spell
In those gray, mediaeval days when Dante sang of hell.
The lean old exile travelled far his shadow-haunted path,
And wrote his book in solitude and ate his heart in wrath.
And everywhere he wandered did the dilettante throng
Deplore the wane of poetry, the sad decay of song.
"Ah, once," they wept, "the Sons of Light did crowd this world about.
The earth was bright with geniuses; but now we are just out."
When Shakespeare ran a theatre, one time in London town,
'Tis said he made good dividends and brought the galleries down.
And many in those London streets looked on this man, perchance.
But no man ever turned his head to get a second glance.
He played old Hamlet's ghost, 'tis said; and thus he spent his days,
A mediocre actor and a tinker of old plays.
And loud they mourned for geniuses, and loud went up the shout:
"Lord send us geniuses once more: for now we are just out."

The Old Emigrant

I

In '48
John Henry Mead,
Erastus White, James Carr,
  Sebastian French,
  Uriah Cass,
Myself and Joseph Farr,
  Did emigrate
  And bring our wives
To this town of Chegung;
  The world was full
  Of love and hope —
For we were young.

  We cleared the woods,
  And through their roots
We drove our breaking plough;
  We sowed the meadows,
  Made the hills
A pasture for the cow;
  We founded firesides
  In the woods.
In this town of Chegung;
  And built glad homes
  Where children played —

For we were young.

We built our mills
Beside the streams,
And through the solitudes
Our whirling saw
In triumph sung
The death song of the woods;
We built the church
Upon the hill
In this town of Chegung;
We worked with God
To make earth glad —
For we were young.

We built the school,
And for its frame
Felled many a tall pine tree;
In hope, we planned
Our sons should grow
Far wiser men than we.
We raised strong boys,
And brave and good,
In this town of Chegung;
We taught them how
To front the world —
For we were young.

II

A mighty town
Down by the sea
Has grown up with Chegung;
And called our boys
And they have gone,
And we're no longer young.
Its towers are high,
Its streets are thronged,
Its vaults are filled with gold;
Its noise and wealth
Have drawn our boys —
And we are old.

Down to the town
Beside the sea
They've gone, and left us here;
And they are young

64

And they are strong,
They know not what is fear.
    The embers fade.
    The fire burns low.
The very sun grows cold;
    And we old men
    Stay here alone —
And we are old.
    God made the young
    To help the old —
The Great Town by the Sea
    Robs us old men
    Of our own boys,
Far stronger men than we.
    But there's a town,
    So we've been taught,
Whose streets are paved with gold,
    And soon once more
    We'll emigrate —
For we are old.

The Life Hunger of William Gulick

Young Billy Gulick used to yearn
    And ceaselessly aspire:
To be the owner of a dog
    Was his supreme desire;
And tow'rd that far transcendent goal
    He kept an endless jog —
Tow'rd that "far-off, divine event "
    When he should own a dog.
He passed through days of blasted hope
    And nights of bitter tears,
And lost the sweetest wine of life
    Through all those dogless years.

But Fate, though sometimes very slow,
    Keeps up her tireless jog,
And in the fulness of her time
    Young Billy found his dog.
But now a grander dream had come
    To through his visions float
And fill the youth's aspiring soul —
    A goat-cart and a goat.
And now no dog, while this new dream

Held him in its control,
  Could satisfy the hunger of
    Young Billy Gulick's soul.

And so the mighty universe
    From its abysms dim
Of boundless possibilities
    Produced a goat for him.
But soon his vision, clarified
    Of its obstructing motes,
Beheld the poor illusiveness
    And vanity of goats.
And now another great desire
    Filled him with zeal profound —
A pony and a pony-cart
    He tied his heart-strings round.

There was no hope, no light, no joy,
    No songs of glad delight;
The world without that pony was
    One black Cimmerian night.
But look! A star breaks through the gloom.
    The universe at need
From its exhaustless latencies
    Produced his pony steed.
Then Billy Gulick felt removed
    Life's pessimistic blight.
His bearing tow'rd the universe
    Grew courteous and polite.

But in a very few short months,
    The unvarnished truth to tell,
His pony-team grew weary, stale,
    Flat and unprofitable.
He dreamed of school and college halls,
    And chose as his pursuit
To climb the tree of knowledge and
    To shake down all its fruit.
He climbed the tree and shook its trunk,
    But yet high over him
Hung tantalizing apples still
    Upon some loftier limb.

But now he dreamed the dream of love;
    The bright star in his skies

66

Was the celestial light that beams
    From out a maiden's eyes.
"But it's no use," poor Billy sighed,
    "She is too fair and far —
Why should a vain, presumptuous worm
    Aspire to a star?"
But none the less the worm aspired
    To that far blessedness,
And when the worm "popped" to the star.
    The star — she answered, "Yes."
Did they live happy? S-h-h! Don't ask;
    All gossip I detest,
And no domestic secrecies
    By me shall be expressed.
Enough, that Billy still did yearn
    And still new goals did find,
With H-o-n. before his name
    And LL.D. behind.
But though he went to Congress as
    His district's special pride,
Yet William Gulick, LL.D.,
    Was still unsatisfied.

But now another mighty dream
    Before his vision floats;
He yearns now for the Presidency
    As once for dogs and goats.
He deems, if in the President's chair
    He once could take his seat.
He'd rest in satisfied content;
    His life would be complete.
But should he reach the Presidency,
    Borne by the people's vote,
'Twould be just like his pony-cart,
    His goat-cart, and his goat.
                * * * * * *
But Billy's but a myth of mine.
    An allegoric blind;
Thou art the man! and so am I,
    And so is all mankind.
We all are Billy Gulicks, for
    Full wide his tribe is spread:
You find a man who's satisfied
    You find a man who's dead.

And if you find a live man who
    For nothing further sighs,
Though in the pink-red bloom of health
    He's dead before he dies.

A Monopolist's Wants

I

My wants are few, I sit serene
    Upon contentment's highlands;
If I can have earth's continents,
    I care not for its islands.
I would not climb upon a throne
    Through seas of bloody slaughter;
If I can call all lands my own,
    Why, you can have the water.

II

Give me but these; they are enough
    To suit my humble notion,
And you can have, for all your own.
    The land beneath the ocean.
And 'tis a generous slice of earth
    And doubtless quite prolific
If you can only drain it once —
    The bed of the Pacific.

III

And all I ask is just this earth,
    To regulate and man it,
And I surrender all my claims
    To every other planet.
And so, you see, I cut my cloth
    On a contracted pattern;
Give me the earth; I drop all claim
    To Uranus and Saturn.

IV

Little I need; my wants are few;
    Nor would I have them greater;
I only want the land between
    The poles and the equator.

Give me the earth, 'tis all I ask
    For me and my wife, Sarah;
Then I'll give all my fellow-men
    A house-lot in Sahara.

V

The earth is very, very small
    And not in good repair;
Compared with Sirius, it is
    A very small affair.
And I just want it while I live.
    And death, — I'll not resist him, —
For after death I hope to get
    The whole great solar system.

The Ten-Thumbed Man

The world goes wrong while on its surface lingers
    The man whose fingers all are awkward thumbs;
The man who has ten thumbs and has no fingers,
    All heaven-born order at his touch succumbs:
Where'er he fumbles furniture quakes,
Where'er he steps the very flooring shakes,
The dishes rattle and the crockery breaks,
    And glass lies strewn about in broken crumbs.

O'er all external nature doth he stumble
    And every object that obstructs his way:
Then tangled with his own feet doth he tumble
    And falleth o'er himself without delay.
His march of triumph gapes with broken walls,
From every fence tumultuously he falls,
Through all the startled scenery he sprawls
    And strews a track of ruin through the day.

The man who has ten thumbs but has no fingers
    He keeps his elbows out in every crowd,
On crazed men's corns his placid foot still lingers,
    And on the silken trains of ladies proud.
The sweet girl's bonnet lies a shapeless mass;
The plate glass window is but broken glass,
Through crushed-out eyes doth his umbrella pass,
    And strong men curse and women weep aloud.

Where'er he goes do brave men flee like rabbits,

Aye, mighty warriors deem it safe to run;
They know his fatal, cataclysmic habits
    And all his havoc wrought beneath the sun.
Where'er he goes is formless chaos brewing,
The cosmos trembles at his own undoing.
And order yields her ancient reign to ruin —
    He blunders on until his work is done.

He joins the club, and straightway fatal faction
    Usurps the place where concord reigned before,
Weaves his ten thumbs in every small transaction.
    And harmony and peace are known no more;
The milk of poetry turns to sour prose,
Through that doomed club hot molten language flows,
The roof reechoes with resounding blows.
    And mangled club-men strew the reeking floor.

Into the church where pious men are banding
    To put down sin and all its deeds goes he,
And then the peace which passeth understanding
    In that doomed church becomes an absentee.
The pastor yields himself to slow despair,
The choir's jangling fills the mangled air,
The deacons fight and tear each other's hair,
    The church disbands, and Satan laughs in glee.

The man who has ten thumbs but has no fingers —
    Domestic peace ne'er sheds its gentle force
Within the fated home where'er he lingers,
    Nor true love wends its unobstructed course.
Within that home there sounds perpetual war,
Discordant noise and altercation raw.
And fluent frenzy fires his mother-in-law,
    And daily prays his wife for a divorce.

I'll sit beside the sneak-thief and am willing
    At the same board to gather up the crumbs.
And I'll embrace with love the vagrant villain
    Who plays on trombones or who beats on drums.
I'll love the fool and tolerate the bore.
Cherish the crank and bless him evermore.
But Fate — kind Fate — divert him from my door -
    The tactless man whose fingers all are thumbs.

Matilda's New Year Resolutions

(Afore I spin my yarn to you
   Right here an' now I wish to pause
An' tell you it is gospel true —
   My wife's the best wife ever was;
Now I have made this plain as day,
I'll spin my yarn and say my say.)

Las' New Year's Day my wife she vowed
   Thet she'd no more unloose the bung
Thet held her temper in an' swowed
   No more she'd bang me with her tongue;
No more she'd em'ty on my path
The roarin' flood-gates of her wrath.

Las' Tuesday wuz a New Year' day,
   Ez calm and sweet ez heaven itself.
I packed all grief an' pain away —
   I packed it on the highes' shelf.
For not one jaw-word did she say
Through all that long an' blessed day.

But Wednesday mornin' she got riled
   Coz I brought mud in on my boots,
An' broke out purty middlin' wild
   In one of her etarnal toots.
An' fired her grape an' blazed away
For purty nigh a half a day.

(An' now afore I tell no more
   I want to make it plump and plain.
So good a wife hain't lived before
   An' one so good won't live again.
Now we hev on this pint agreed
I'll take my yarn up and perceed.)

Nex' day I spilt pie on my vest
   (She is the boss at makin' pie);
She said I wuz the dirtiest
   Ol' sloven an' deserved to die.
A man who couldn' eat punkin pie
'Thout slobberin' roun' deserved to die.

An' then her wild volcaner broke,
   An' she belched forth for half a day,

71

An' filled the atmosphere with smoke
    In her own old peculiar way.
I grabbed my overcoat in fright,
Skun out an' didn' come back till night.
(An' now right here 'fore I perceed
    I want it plainly understood
My wife she allus takes the lead
    In all things thet are sweet an' good;
An' I want you to understand
Thet she's the best wife in the land.)

Las' Friday night I broke a lamp,
    An' she came down upon me then,
An' called me lubber, lummux, scamp,
    The mos' outrageous gawk of men;
An' took a piece of ol' sink lead
An' banged me with it on the head.

(Now jest hol' on a minute here —
    I wish to say right here an' now,
There ain't no wife so sweet an' dear
    As my good wife, Matilda Howe.
An' now on this we're both agreed,
Once more I'm ready to perceed.)

With this sink lead she laid me out,
    I fainted an' grew deathly pale,
An' yes'day mornin' Sheriff Strout
    He took Matilda off to jail;
Wounded and sick I languish here
Without her tender care to cheer.

But I won't yield to grief an' doubt,
    An' to Matilda I'll be true.
Nex' New Year's Day will she git out,
    An' we'll begin our life anew.
(An' now I'll say before I pause,
She is the best wife ever was.)

The Feats and Falls of John Bean

Once in the jungles of Brazil
A cougar, with intent to kill,
Leaped at John Bean upon his right
With eyes on fire — a fearful sight!

An alligator, with his jaws
Extended wide as they could be,
Without a single moment's pause
Upon his left yawned viciously;
A boa constrictor from a limb
Above his head then leaped at him.
A fearful moment! for all three
Leaped at him simultaneously.
The alligator, cougar, snake,
All leaped together. Calm, serene,
As peaceful as a sleeping lake.
Stood imperturbable John Bean
Then with a hand that did not fail,
He seized the long snake by the tail.
And midway pulled him o'er the limb,
And there he deftly balanced him.
Then tied the tail with lightning haste
Around the alligator's waist;
Then tied the head all panting warm
Around the cougar's wriggling form.
The long snake hung there — sight of dread!
He hung there swinging in the gale,
The alligator at his head,
The cougar dangling at his tail —
They hung there, swinging like a sweep,
While John lay down and went to sleep.
All this is sober truth, I know,
For John himself he told me so.

In Indian deeps without a plank
John floated on the sea,
Ten days he swam and never sank,
Till he a whale did see.
He met the whale in deadly strife,
And killed it with his stout jack-knife.
He took its skin for a balloon.
Inflated it with careful toil,
With hot air he procured soon
By burning the whale's oil.
In this balloon then high and grand,
John floated off till he found land.
And all this tale is strictly true —
For John told me, and I tell you.

When John came home from wanderings far,

In every land, 'neath every star.
His feats all previous feats did dim,
And we were very proud of him —
For he who shows a lion fine
Himself is reckoned leonine.

But if John wandered off alone,
He'd come back with some broken bone;
And he'd return all dislocated
With hands, or arms, or feet mismated.
   When he went out we felt a dread
      As we beheld him through the gate,
    Lest he'd come home without his head
      Or in some fragmentary state.
For while he talked of fearsome feats
   With monsters on the land or sea,
In all the manholes in the streets
   He'd fall with perilous accuracy.
And with a fateful instinct sure
He fell in every open sewer;
And every time a snow-slide hit.
He was the fellow under it.
   His talk — a symphony of events
      Of wonder that all wonder dims;
   His acts — a string of accidents —
      A discord of disrupted limbs.

Once when he told about a shark
That chased him round from dawn till dark,
And how he put the shark to rout
By shinning up a waterspout,
A street steam-roller caught the sinner
And rolled him some five inches thinner.

One day he told us in a mine
   He once was buried when asleep,
Without a single warning sign,
   Two thousand and some odd feet deep.
And then a wonder came to pass
   Such as we read of in romances —
He pierced the superincumbent mass
   With one of his keen, piercing glances.
His glance shot through the wall about
And through the fissure he walked out.
But while he told this wondrous tale

He stumbled o'er a street-car rail,
Became entangled with the car
And cracked a dorsal vertebra.

Some quarrymen he tried to tell
How in Vesuvius he fell,
And sat him down — a fearful sight!
Upon a can of dynamite.
They listened to the great narrator
And learned how he fell in the crater.
But evermore remained in doubt
As to the manner he got out;
For though he was full primed and loaded
The can of dynamite exploded —
He shot up like a mounting lark
And made no subsequent remark.
　　　　* * * * * *
We tried to have a funeral,
　　We did our best — but fate was rough —
We had no funeral at all,
　　We couldn't collect remains enough.

Odium Theologicum

They met and they talked where the cross-roads meet,
Four men from the four winds come,
And they talked of the horse, for they loved the theme,
And never a man was dumb
And the man from the North loved the strength of the horse.
And the man from the East his pace,
And the man from the South loved the speed of the horse,
The man from the West his grace.

So these four men from the four winds come.
Each paused a space in his course
And smiled in the face of his fellow-man
And lovingly talked of the horse.
Then each man parted and went his way
As their different courses ran;
And each man journeyed with peace in his heart
And loving his fellow-man.

II

They met the next year where the cross-roads meet,

Four men from the four winds come;
And it chanced as they met that they talked of God,
    And never a man was dumb.
One imaged God in the shape of a man,
    A spirit did one insist;
One said that Nature itself was God,
    One said that He didn't exist.

But they lashed each other with tongues that stung,
    That smote as with a rod:
Each glared in the face of his fellow-man,
    And wrathfully talked of God.
Then each man parted and went his way.
    As their different courses ran:
And each man journeyed with war in his heart.
    And hating his fellow-man.

The Shuttlecock Cry of The Heart

We wish to come back with as fervid desire
    As ever we wish to depart:
"I want to go somewhere," "I want to get back,"
    Is the shuttlecock cry of the heart.

When the high tide of summer breaks over the year
    We would float on its flowery crest
Till it leaves us adrift on the pine-covered hills,
    Or the buttercup valleys of rest.

But the sad winds of autumn, like wandering cries,
    Seem the voices of spirits that roam,
And they echo our thoughts through the deepening skies,
    Our longing and hunger for home.

And blesséd are they who return to their homes —
    As blesséd as they who depart:
"I want to go somewhere," " I want to get back,"
    Is the shuttlecock cry of the heart.

June

"God geometrizes," does he? So old Plato said, and you
Must admit that this man Plato used to know a thing or two.

God geometrizes, Plato? Beg your pardon; but I grieve

To protest that this, your statement, I sincerely disbelieve.
Ah, God poetizes, Plato, in this high, June-tide of flowers,
With the rhythm of his rose banks, and the metre of his showers.

Does God build by lines and angles? Seek and search you far and near!
Where the rounded hills are flushing with the strong wine of the year.

Where the tangled vines o'ercluster every hill and mountain pass,
And the emerald meadows shimmer with the greenery of the grass.

Hear ye not the primal music of the morning stars in tune?
For old Adam's earliest Eden visits earth with every June.

And the deathless life that winter in his icy chains had curled,
Breaks in strong, tumultuous music from the glad heart of the world.

And the brook, a wandering poet, all the air with music fills.
And he sings to listening meadows all the lyrics of the hills.

Plato, Plato, mighty Grecian, all the after years have wrought
Great philosophies and systems from the quarry of thy thought;

All the world in seeking wisdom back to thee has gazed behind,
And thou sittest, crowned with Shakespeare, as the greatest of mankind.

But thy reason was not flawless — may there not be room to doubt —
When you dreamed your great " Republic " drove you not the poets out?

But God poetizes, Plato: and his thought flows into tune —
And the climax of his music is the longest day in June.

A New Year's Parable

I AM free to confess I am under the law
Of both Biddy McGee and of Billy McGaw;
And Biddy McGee has no folly or flaw,
But a scamp of a rascal is Billy McGaw;
And both Billy McGaw and Biddy McGee
Are parts of the nature that constitute me.

Though Biddy McGee has never a flaw
She's in love with that rascally Billy McGaw:
And Billy McGaw, though he's bad as can be,
He does some tall courting with Biddy McGee;
And both Billy McGaw and Biddy McGee

77

Dwell happy together and constitute me.

But Biddy each New Year's arises in awe
And repulses the rascally Billy McGaw;
And Billy McGaw from her presence doth flee, -
From the virtuous scorn of his Biddy McGee;
And for a brief season, you plainly may see.
Sweet Biddy McGee alone constitutes me.

But the day after New Year's doth Billy McGaw
Hang round in the distance her notice to draw;
And she coyly looks out of the side of her eyes,
And she holds down her head and she blushes and sighs;
The next day he comes and with dignified awe
She addresses him coldly as "Mister McGaw."

He comes the next day, and he sits down to chat.
And she takes his coat and his cane and his hat;
And henceforward they live in a peace without flaw,
Sweet Biddy McGee and bad Billy McGaw.
And bad Billy McGaw and sweet Biddy McGee
This new year, as usual, will constitute me.

Ellen's Ultimatum

"I see you have a tall hat, John;
    I thought that you despised 'em.
I never heard a man run on
    The way you criticised 'em."
"Oh, yes; but Ellen said," quoth John,
    "And said it plain and flat,
A beau to suit her must have on
    A stylish stove-pipe hat;
I wished to suit her as her beau
And bought a stove-pipe hat, you know."

"I see, too, you've a diamond ring;
    But once you used to swear
It was an ostentatious thing
    No modest man should wear."
"That was my former view," said John,
    "But years new wisdom bring,
And Ellen said I must put on
    At least one diamond ring;
I had no courage to demur.
And so I wear the ring for her."

"Your silver watch has been replaced,
   I notice, by a gold one,
A gold one elegantly chased —
   Much better than your old one.
You used to say a watch of gold
   Was useless ostentation " —
"I've changed," said John, "as I've grown old,
   My point of observation;
For Ellen no coarse man would wed
Who wore a silver watch, she said."

"I see you've changed your former shoes
   For those of patent leather —
A kind you swore you'd never use
   While nature held together."
"Don't quote," said John, "my former views;
   'Tis useless to restate 'em;
I bought these patent-leather shoes
   At Ellen's ultimatum;
She vowed no husband she would choose
Who wore plain, common-leather shoes."

"Now you and Ellen soon will wed?"
   At this did John turn yellow.
"Why, she's run off," he sadly said,
   "And with another fellow."
"How did this other fellow dress,
   What did the man have on? "
"Slouch hat, brass ring, brass watch — and, yes —
   Old cowhide boots," said John;
"Old cowhide boots, brass watch, brass ring.
Slouch hat and all that sort of thing."

Modern Degeneracy

I've just been reading in a book I think is gospel true,
That men are now degenerate. Well, that is nothing new.
I've been aware for several years the race is going to grass;
I've prophesied it night and day — and now it's come to pass.

Now, I've sold milk for forty years, and I can truly say.
Before men grew degenerate the milk trade used to pay;
A man who had good business sense and honest business ways
Could make a fortune out of milk in those old honest days.

I loved my customers — I did — a love that was divine;
No milk to ever injure them came from a can of mine.
A cow is a most ignorant beast, with small supply of brain,
And no mere unassisted cow can give good milk, 'tis plain.

My intellect supplied the lack of the unreasoning cow;
I finished her unfinished milk — my reason told me how.
An unassisted cow gives milk too rich for men to drink;
A man must supplement the cow, for he knows how to think.

I made a study of the thing and well I understood
A cow's raw undiluted milk's too rich for human food;
And so I toned its richness down and mellowed every can
To the digestive calibre and wholesome needs of man.

And my astute discernment as to what man could digest,
My prudence toward my customers, my kindly interest,
My interference with the cow in the behalf of health —
All helped toward my prosperity and my increase of wealth.

But those were undegenerate days. Though God made man upright.
He has sought out vain inventions and has reached a sorry plight.
A creamery started in our town, and in these modern days
Does that monopolistic shark gulp all the milk we raise.

And it runs it through a strainer then that separates the cream,
And they just pay us for the cream — a most outrageous scheme —
And all the water you put in is industry misspent;
For all the water in the milk you don't receive a cent.

We live in base, ignoble times, we're fallen on evil days;
I cannot modernize myself to these degenerate ways;
The vain inventions of our time fill me with righteous rage.
There is no place for honest men in this degenerate age.

Abraham and Ephraim

He sermonized industriously in his didactic way,
And moralized momentously with Ephraim every day,
And taught by tale and proverb and by every good device
The virtuousness of virtue and the viciousness of vice.
His hortatory homilies, intended to impress
The rightfulness of righteousness, the sin of sinfulness,
Were ever hurled at Ephraim throughout the whole year long,

That he might rightly comprehend the wrongfulness of wrong.

"A youth can grow up virtuous, if we but pay the price;
If we but saturate his soul with showers of advice;
If we instill," said Abraham, "perpetual truth in him — "
And so in truth perpetually he soaked young Ephraim.

The youth absorbed a sermon every morning ere he ate
On the awful reprobation of the awful reprobate;
And he swallowed moral theses that were meant to edify,
And he masticated maxims with his gingerbread and pie.

And 'twixt breakfast time and dinner the iniquity of sin
Was taught to him industriously and patiently rubbed in;
The turpidness of turpitude was duly analyzed
And the evil of depravity was loudly advertised.

And then right after dinner the enormity of crime
And the wrong of immorality was preached till supper time.
Then Abraham would sermonize through all the evening hours,
And drench young Ephraim's consciousness in moralistic showers.

Thus through cumulative precept did old Abraham desire
Accumulative virtue should young Ephraim acquire;
He taught him virtue endlessly, and waited long to see
How superlatively virtuous young Ephraim would be.

Thus maxim goaded Ephraim found righteousness a bore,
For salve is but an irritant when jammed into a sore;
Even bread is innutritious if you resolutely cram
An indiscriminate bakery down the bursting diaphragm.

Thus by hortatory homilies did Abraham impress
The wrongfulness of righteousness, the good of sinfulness;
And taught by tale and proverb and by every good device.
The viciousness of virtue and the virtuousness of vice.

Hence, Ephraim lived a reckless life and died a felon's death,
But gave this vindication with his latest dying breath:
"I have been sermonized to death; I die, to speak precise.
An unprotected victim of perpetual advice."

Contentment

Through the valleys of Ridge,
    Over hilltops and plain,
Through dust you could cut
    Did we rush for the train;
And we came, Tom and I,
    To the station at last
Just in time to behold
    The long train rolling past.
But Tom smiled his brave smile,
    And said: "I don't care;
I have the same head on my shoulders in Ridge
    That I have on my shoulders in Weare.

"I have the same head
    And can think the same thought
In the thunder of London
    Or Brown's pasture-lot;
And under all skies
    And beneath every star
'Tis not where you live,
    But the man that you are.
So I'll sit here and wait
    Like a man without care;
I have the same heart in my bosom in Ridge
    That I have in my bosom in Weare.

"And with cheer in your heart
    And with sense in your brain
You can get to your depot
    Without any train;
And you can't buy a train
    With unlimited pelf
That will carry a mortal
    Outside of himself.
And he takes his own demon
    And saint everywhere;
He has the same man in his jacket in Ridge
    That he has in his jacket in Weare.

"No express trains that whiz
    Through the land with a breeze,
And no vessels that sail
    On the limitless seas,

Though they cross the equator
    And make for the pole.
Can bear a man's body
    Away from his soul.
Though I miss every train,
    Yet I'll never despair:
I have the same soul in my body in Ridge
    That I have in my body in Weare.

"The same head, the same heart,
    The same man, the same soul.
On this side the ocean,
    Or that side the pole;
And no engine or ship,
    In no climate or zone,
Can bear any mortal
    Away from his own.
Though I wait for the train,
    Yet I'll sturdily bear
The same sweet content in my being in Ridge
    That I bear in my being in Weare."

Jack Cleaves' Conservatism

"Give me old truths," said Lemuel Cleaves; " in them will I abide;
Old truths made strong by test of years, by custom sanctified.

"Give me old views the fathers held, by long years made sublime,
And sacred with the sanctity of immemorial time.

"Hold fast the old, distrust the new, and endless battle wage
With the iconoclastic trend of this destructive age.

"Truth sanctioned by the sages and the thinkers of the past
Is strong enough and good enough and true enough to last.

"Why cast aside these olden truths, in honored years grown gray.
For the fripperies and foolishness and foibles of today?"

Coeval with his ancestors did Lemuel make life's trip,
But with his own contemporaries had no companionship.

II

And Lemuel had a son, Jack Cleaves, whom he proposed to teach
The old truths — keeping all the new forever from his reach.

And so he took the hopeful lad and taught him day by day
To comprehend that ancient truth that A is simply A.

"That's A," would Lemuel persist, and Jack would lift his eyes
For many long successive weeks in ever new surprise.

"That's A, my boy," and Jack would feel a pleasure unconfined
As the freshness of this ancient truth broke in upon his mind.

"That's A," day after day he said, and still the raptured youth
Drank in the sacred grandeur of this immemorial truth.

And Jack still loved this old, old truth, and hastened every day
To hear his father demonstrate the truth that A was A.

III

Then, after many studious months, his father thought the youth
Had reached an intellectual strength to stand another truth.

"Now, here's another letter, Jack, which I wish you to see;
Apply your intellectual powers and learn that this is B."

" Give me the old, old truths," said Jack, " for I would always stay
In the sacred contemplation of the truth that A is A.

" Why cast aside those olden truths in honored years grown gray
For the fripperies and the foolishness and foibles of to-day?

"With this newfangled letter, pa, why should we longer stay?
Give me the old, old truth again, and talk to me of A."

The Tale of Hiram Hale

Then you want to hear a story that is true and realistic?
One that isn't psychologic, neither marvellous nor mystic?
  Then hear my tale
  Of Hiram Hale.
No shooting pyrotechnics and no lime -light coruscation,
And no phosphorescent fire-shine glimmer in this true narration —
  You'll like this tale
  Of Hiram Hale.
There was nothing supereminent or superfine in Hiram,
For he was the son of Susan and also of Adoniram;
  Fair, every day

Plain folks, they say.
His wife was not illustrious, but very much like Hiram,
The daughter of his neighbors, Ruth and Abraham Abiram.
        Five children came
        About the same.
The universe beheld their deeds and never got excited,
The river that flowed by their house they none of them ignited:
        It flowed by it
        And kept unlit.
What's that you say? You think this tale a wretched imposition?
And as a story-telling bard I've surely missed my mission?
        My tale falls flat?
        Why, how is that?
Oh, "no elopements, suicides, or red assassination?
No villain and no crisis, no dramatic culmination
        No love's rough course,
        And no divorce."
Why, Hiram was industrious and fairly conscientious,
And led a mainly honest life, correct and unpretentious;
        What ails this tale
        Of Hiram Hale?
When you can get integrity you do not want venality.
And when I tell of honesty you cannot wish rascality.
        You do? Oh, no.
        It can't be so.
What forgeries and robberies and crimes more entertaining
Than this true tale of Hiram Hale of which you are complaining?
        Why, I'm surprised!
        And scandalized!
An honest man who does his work and labors long and willing
Is not so entertaining as a good professional villain?
        I'm scandalized
        And sore surprised!

It Stuck in His Crop

There is too little corn, an' too much husk an' cob,
    An' it sticks in my crop,
And folks that work hardes' git least fer their job,
    An' it sticks in my crop.
It takes a big tree to perduce a small cherry,
An' it needs a large bush for a tarnal small berry.
An' a man must git wealthy afore he can merry,
    An' it sticks in my crop.

There is mighty small taters an' mighty big weeds,
    An' it sticks in my crop,
An' too big perfessions an' too httle deeds.
    An' it sticks in my crop.
An' there's too little readin' in too many pages.
An' too little wisdom in too many sages,
An' the men who work hardes' they git the least wages, —
An' it sticks in my crop.

An' the men who earn bread by the sweat of their brow
    (It sticks in my crop)
Git the wust kin' er bread that there is, anyhow,
    An' it sticks in my crop:
But the men who dress up like a dude or a dandy,
They eat nothin' worser than puddin' or candy,
An' they reach out an' grab jest w'atever comes handy, —
    An' it sticks in my crop.

An' the poor man, like me, who digs in the dirt
    (It sticks in my crop),
Never wears a tailed coat, never wears a biled shirt,
    An' it sticks in my crop:
But them swell chaps who never do toilin' nor spinnin'.
But divide up their time betwixt sleepin' and sinnin'.
Go aroun', like men-peacocks, in purple an' linen —
    An' it sticks in my crop:

It sticks in my crop, I can't swaller it down,
    It sticks in my crop.
That the hard-workin' woman must wear a coarse gown,
    It sticks in my crop;
While the gals who're too nice fer to let the ol' cat in,
An' all study music, an' paintin' an' Latin,
Never wear nothin' poorer than sealskin an' satin,
    An' it sticks in my crop.

An' it sticks in my crop thet me an' my wife
    Gosh, it sticks in my crop,
Hev pressed sour juice from the winepress er life.
    Ah, it sticks in my crop;
Fate seems ter delight just ter kick us an' cuff us,
An' the worl' doesn't care how much either one suffers,
If we jaw, it exclaims, "What ungrateful ol' duffers,"
    An' it sticks in my crop.

Work

The Fiend that harries the souls of men
    Came up from his lowest hell
To, fiendlike, play with the soul of a man
    That he had pondered well.
The soul of a man serene and strong,
Who had worked in joy his whole life long.
And who loved his work, as a strong man should.
And looked on his work and called it good.

    And he smote from the man his friends. They turned
        From his daily haunts and ways.
    And they passed him by with a look of hate
        Or with an averted gaze.
Then the friendless man, in his life apart,
On the love of his labor fed his heart.
And in the joy of his work no more
Remembered the scorn of his friends of yore.

    And he smote from the man his love. The heart
        He had cherished as his own
    Crew false to his love that was strong as life,
        And the man was left alone.
Then the loveless man choked down his tears
And worked through the gloom of the lonely years;
With the dragon shapes of his grief he fought,
Upheld by the love of the work he wrought.

    And he smote from the man his fame. The praise
        Of his youth came not again,
    And his name, that had blown about the world,
        Was dead on the lips of men.
Then the fameless man, with his dead renown.
Grew faint with the weight of his iron crown;
But he turned to his work as a strong retreat
And forgot the shame of his great defeat.
    Then the Fiend that harries the souls of men,
        In the strength of a hate untold,
    Despoiled the man of his power to work, —
        And the heart of the man grew old;
And he raised his hands to the pitiless sky.
And he prayed to the heavens for the power to die.
And the Fiend grew glad and he laughed, "'Tis well";
And then he returned to his lowest hell.

Tad Bowers' Prayer

At Taggart's mine in '49 the men were rough and reckless,
And no immaculate men were there and none whose souls were speckless.
The picked and sifted perfect man is somewhat hard to see, —
At Taggart's mine in '49 he was an absentee.

Some came on borrowed horses, loaned without their owner's knowledge;
And ninety-nine had been to jail to one who'd been to college —
Men free to talk on various themes with all who'd give them credence.
But swathed in sacred silentness about their antecedents.

At Bowers' shanty they didn't read Dante, or meditate on Kant,
And intellectual pursuits you might admit were scant,
But down to Bowers' the evening hours were spent in pastimes light.
Each night the men begun with cards and ended with a fight.

And in a broil like this one night did Bowers' five-year Tad,
A blue- eyed boy with flaxen curls, a sturdy, roguish lad,—
His father's pistol take, in play, and swing it round his head, —
The charge by accident went off, and Hank Malone dropped dead.

"That imp. Tad Bowers," cried Hank's old pard,
"has murdered Hank Malone,
I see him shoot, the little brute! the crime he can't disown.
Now take him out, an' string him up, and lift him high an' dry.
In cold blood he has killed my pard, the little wretch mus' die!"

"Yes, take him out an' string him up!" yelled those half- drunken men,
"We'll send the imp at double quick where he won't shoot again.
Sam Flint, we've made you sheriff here: Now show what you can do,
We've got a hanging on our hands, we give the job to you."

"Come, boy," said Sam, "the time has come that I must stop your fun.
And now, my young kid, now I guess, that all your pranks are done."
The little lad was wild with fear, and sought his father's arm, —
A refuge that should never fail to guard a child from harm.

The maudlin father, dazed with drink, he could not comprehend,
And so the lad was snatched away and told to meet his end.
"An' tan I say a 'ittle prayer my mama teached to me?"
"Yes, say your foolishness," said Sam, — "and then we'll find a tree."

"Now — I lay me — down to s'eep," the curly lad began —
It seemed a bolt had cleft the heavens and struck each gazing man.
I p'ay — the Lord — my — soul to teep," he sobbed between his tears,

And each man saw a trundle bed loom through the mist of years.

"If I should die — before I wake" — the trundle bed stood clear,
And mother's sweet and blessed face was bending down to hear.
"I p'ay the Lord my soul to take " — the little prayer was said,
And each man felt his mother's breath above his trundle bed.

"An' now I'se weady," said the lad. The sheriff said,
"I ain't,
An' if you're lookin' for a man to kill that little saint,
You must get another sheriff," and he choked a rising sob,
"You must git another sheriff, for I will not do the job!"

"To-morrer if that boy is dead no man should live an' thrive.
An' I, for one, would be ashamed to find myself alive!
An' if there's killin' to be done, I want you men to see.
Before you kill thet urchin there you've got to first kill me."

"Three cheers for ol' Sam Flint! " they cried.
    "Three cheers for little Tad! "
And ev'ry grizzly whiskered man bent down and kissed the lad,
And the old pard of Hank Malone came forward with the rest,
And little Tad leaped in his arms and nestled on his breast.

The Meeting of The Clabberhuses

I

He was the Chairman of the Guild
    Of Early Pleiocene Patriarchs;
He was chief Mentor of the Lodge
    Of the Oracular Oligarchs.
He was the Lord High Autocrat
    And Vizier of the Sons of Light,
And Sultan and Grand Mandarin
    Of the Millennial Men of Might.

He was Grand Totem and High Priest
Of the Independent Potentates;
Grand Mogul of the Galaxy
Of the Illustrious Stay-out-lates;
The President of the Dandydudes,
The Treasurer of the Sons of Glee:
The Leader of the Clubtown Band
And Architects of Melody.

II

She was Grand Worthy Prophetess
    Of the Illustrious Maids of Mark;
Of Vestals of the Third Degree
    She was Most Potent Matriarch;
She was High Priestess of the Shrine
    Of Clubtown's Culture Coterie,
And First Vice-President of the League
    Of the Illustrious G. A. B.

She was the First Dame of the Club
    For Teaching Patagonians Greek;
She was Chief Clerk and Auditor
    Of Clubtown's Anti-Bachelor Clique:
She was High Treasurer of the Fund
    For Borrioboolaghalians,
And the Fund for Sending Browning's Poems
    To Native-born Australians.

III

Once to a crowded social fete
    Both these much-titled people came,
And each perceived, when introduced.
    They had the self-same name.
Their hostess said, when first they met:
    "Permit me now to introduce
My good friend Mr. Clabberhuse
    To Mrs. Clabberhuse."

"'Tis very strange," said she to him,
    "Such an unusual name.
A name so very seldom heard.
    That we should bear the same."
"Indeed, 'tis wonderful," said he
    "And I'm surprised the more,
Because I never heard the name
    Outside my home before.

"But now I come to look at you,"
Said he, "upon my life,
If I am not indeed deceived.
You are — you are — my wife."
She gazed into his searching face
And seemed to look him through;

90

"Indeed," said she, "it seems to me
You are my husband, too.

"I've been so busy with my clubs
And in my various spheres
I have not seen you now," she said,
" For over fourteen years."
" That's just the way it's been with me.
These clubs demand a sight" —
And then they both politely bowed.
And sweetly said "Good night."

Miracles

Since I have listened to the song
    The melted snow-bank sings,
I've roamed the earth a credulous man,
    Believing many things.
The snow which made the mountains white
    Made green the babbling lea;
And since that day have miracles
    Been commonplace to me.

Sprung from the slime of sluggish streams.
    Inert, and dark, and chilly,
Have I not seen the miracle
    And glory of the lily?
Have I not seen, when June's glad smile
    Upon the earth reposes,
The cosmic impulse in the clod
    Reveal itself in roses?

Have I not seen the frozen hill,
    Where snowy chaos tosses.
Smile back upon the smiling sun
    With violets and mosses?
Have I not seen the dead old world
    Rise to a newer birth,
When fragrance from the lilac blooms
    Rejuvenates the earth?

Have I not seen the rolling earth,
    A clod of frozen death.
Burst from its grave-clothes of the snow
    Touched by an April breath?

Have I not seen the bare-boughed tree,
    That from the winter shrinks,
Imparadised in apple blooms
    And loud with bobolinks?

Now who can riddle me this thing?
    Or tell me how or where
The tulip stains its crimson cup
    From the transparent air?
So from the wonder-bearing day
    I take the gifts it brings,
And roam the earth a credulous man.
    Believing many things.

The Bloodless Sportsman

" Hast thou named all the birds without a gun?
Loved the wood- rose and left it on its stalk?"
Emerson.

I go a-gunning, but take no gun;
    I fish without a pole;
And I bag good game and catch such fish
    As suit a sportsman's soul;
For the choicest game that the forest holds,
    And the best fish of the brook,
Are never brought down by a rifle shot
    And never are caught with a hook.

I bob for fish by the forest brook,
    I hunt for game in the trees,
For bigger birds than wing the air
    Or fish that swim the seas.
A rodless Walton of the brooks
    A bloodless sportsman, I —
I hunt for the thoughts that throng the woods.
    The dreams that haunt the sky.

The woods were made for the hunters of dreams,
    The brooks for the fishers of song;
To the hunters who hunt for the gunless game
    The streams and the woods belong.
There are thoughts that moan from the soul of the pine,
    And thoughts in a flower bell curled;
And the thoughts that are blown with the scent of the fern
    Are as new and as old as the world.
So, away! for the hunt in the fern-scented wood

Till the going down of the sun;
There is plenty of game still left in the woods
    For the hunter who has no gun.
So, away! for the fish in the moss-bordered brook
    That flows through the velvety sod;
There are plenty of fish still left in the streams
    For the angler who has no rod.

Wen' A Feller Is Out of a Job

All nature is sick from her heels to her hair
    W'en a feller is out of a job,
She is all out of kilter an' out of repair
    W'en a feller is out of a job.
Ain't no juice in the earth an' no salt in the sea,
Ain't no ginger in life in this land of the free,
An' the universe ain't what it's cracked up to be
    W'en a feller is out of a job.

Wat's the good of blue skies an' of blossomin' trees
    W'en a feller is out of a job;
Wen yer boy hez large patches on both of his knees.
    An' a feller is out of a job?
Them patches, I say, look so big to yer eye
That they shet out the lan'scape an' cover the sky,
An' the sun can't shine through 'em the best it can try
    W'en a feller is out of a job.

W'en a man has no part in the work of the earth,
    W'en a feller is out of a job,
He feels the whole blund'rin' mistake of his birth
Wen a feller is out of a job.
He feels he's no share in the whole of the plan,
That he's got the mitten from Natur's own han',
That he's a rejected an' left-over man,
    Wen a feller is out of a job.

For you've jest lost yer holt with the rest of the crowd
    Wen a feller is out of a job;
An' you feel like a dead man with nary a shroud,
    Wen a feller is out of a job.
You are crawlin' aroun' but yer out of the game.
You may bustle about — but yer dead jest the same —
Yer dead with no tombstone to puff up yer name.
    Wen a feller is out of a job.

Ev'ry man that's a man wants to help push the world,
    But he can't if he's out of a job;
He is left out behind, on the shelf he is curled.
    Wen a feller is out of a job.
Ain't no juice in the earth an' no salt in the sea,
Ain't no ginger in life in this land of the free,
An' the universe ain't what it's cracked up to be
    Wen a feller is out of a job.

The Postmistress of Pokumville

That dude down in Chepatchetville,
    He's writin' twice a day
Love-letters nigh a half inch thick
    To young Matilda Pray.
An' Miriam Fitz she has two beaus.
    An' this is solemn true,
One hez his letters pos'marked " Pike,"
    The other " Kalamazoo."
Sich things ez this they pain my soul
    An' worry near to kill;
For I'm postmistress, as you know,
    Down here in Pokumville.

An' 'Rastus Perkins gits a dun
    From Peltenham & Pack
Mos' ev'ry week an' sometimes twice
    For his wife's seal-skin sacque.
An' Martha French — the stuck-up thing!
    With all her lace and frills
Is gettin' duns, from Trask, each month
    For three years' bonnet bills.
Sich things ez these distress the heart,
    Wear out the soul and kill;
For I'm postmistress an' I bear
    The sins of Pokumville.

An' t'other day, O, what a shock!
    Did Deacon Angevine
Git letters from Parnell & Payne,
    "Importers of choice wine."
An' yestiddy — I hate to say,
    What my own eyes have seen,
A matrimonial bureau sent
    A note to Elder Green.

Sometimes w'en I assort the mail
    The shock will almost kill,
To see the wickedness thet's done
    Down here in Pokumville.

An' so I'm worrited to death
    'Bout Bascom's flour bill,
An' 'bout how Seriphina Jones
    Comes on with her beau, Will.
An' lest good Deacon Angevine
    Shall fall away from grace.
An' lest our Elder Green shall bring
    A new wife to the place.
I carry all their woes myself,
    A burden fit to kill.
I feel responserble for all
    The folks of Pokumville.

I work as hard as I can work,
    The best that I can do,
'Tis half-past nine afore I git
    The postal cards read through.
An' w'en Orinthy writes to John
    Or Susan writes to Ned,
I rack my brains in wonderin'
    Jest w'at them gals hev said.
I think if I do not resign,
    This awful work will kill.
An' then a new postmistress here
    Will reign in Pokumville.

The Angel of Discontent

When the world was formed and the morning stars
    Upon their paths were sent,
The loftiest-browed of the angels was made
    The Angel of Discontent.

And he dwelt with man in the caves of the hills,
    Where the crested serpent stings
And the tiger tears and the she-wolf howls, —
    And he told of better things.

And he led man forth to the towered town,
    And forth to the fields of corn;

And told of the ampler work ahead
    For which his race was born.

And he whispers to men of those hills he sees
    In the blush of the misty west:
And they look to the heights of his lifted eye —
    And they hate the name of rest.

In the light of that eye doth the slave behold
    A hope that is high and brave;
And the madness of war comes into his blood —
    For he knows himself a slave.

The serfs of wrong by the light of that eye
    March with victorious songs;
For the strength of the right comes into their hearts
    When they behold their wrongs.

And 'tis by the light of that lifted eye
    That Error's mists are rent:
A guide to the tablelands of Truth
    Is the Angel of Discontent.

And still he looks with his lifted eye,
And his glance is far away
On a light that shines on the glimmering hills
Of a diviner day.

Sambo's Heredity

"Sambo, you stole a watermelon
    Last night, from my back yard.
The punishment for such a felon
    Should be severe and hard."
"Indeed, I's berry sorry, berry,
    But I is not to blame;
My stealun is heredutery,
    My granny did de same.
My granny on meh mudder's side
Stole watermillions till she died."

"But, Sambo, you're a noted liar —
    That mare you sold to me
And said she was a famous flyer
    Is slow as she can be."
"But I is not to blame fer lyin';

My fader alius lied,
An' alius kep' er falserfyin'
    Until de day he died.
An' doan' yo' blame me, Massa Jim,
Fer I inherut it f 'um him."

"Last Thursday, Sambo, you were hired
    To hoe my corn for me,
But now I learn that you were tired
    And slept beneath a tree."
"Now, Massa Jim, doan' yo' git bitter,
    Dat tree wuz splen'id shade —
Meh mudder wuz de laziest critter
    De good Lawd ebber made;
So lazy she couldn' skasely stir.
An' I inherut it f'um her."

"Two rooms you whitewashed last September,
    But I'm obliged to state
You charged, as you can well remember,
    You charged me, sir, for eight."
"I 'fess dat wuz a dreffle cheat, sah,
    But, de good Lawd be praised!
Meh uncle wuz de wust dead-beat, sah,
    Dat Georgy ebber raised;
An' so I ain't to blame, Marse Jim,
T'ank heaven, I 'herut it fum him."

"Ah, Sambo, you're a base deceiver.
    But sometimes you are true;
You nursed my brother in his fever
    And bravely pulled him through.
It was a brave, heroic action,
    From what ancestor, now.
Did you inherit this transaction?"
    And Sambo raised his brow:
"I'll 'fess, sah, fair an' squar' an' flat,
Dat I was 'sponserble fer dat."

A Bottle of Ink

I

A man once bought a bottle of ink
To write the thoughts that he might think.

97

A marble table then he bought
Whereon to write the thoughts he thought.

He bought a farm, fringed round with wood,
Encompassed round with solitude,

That he, where none molest, might sink
And write the thoughts he thought he'd think.

And then around his bottle of ink
He built a house wherein to think;

And in the house he built a room
Retired in dim scholastic gloom;

A room made up of alcoved nooks
And furnished with ten thousand books!

For from such lakes of lore to drink,
He thought would aid his brain to think.

II

His hair was thick and richly brown
When at his desk he sat him down,
And long he gazed within the brink
Of that potential bottle of ink;

Ah, long before it did he stay,
Until his hair was thin and gray!

And dreamed, before that bottle of ink.
Of thoughts he thought he ought to think.

Ah, long he tried to be a bard —
But found his rooster crowed too hard.

And with loud cock-a-doodle-doos
It frightened off the bashful Muse.

He meditated sounding lines —
But the loud winds among the pines

Disturbed him blowing from the west.
And kept his fine lines unexpressed.

And so he died, old, lame, and blind,
And left his bottle of ink behind;

And some one wrote with it a very
Pathetic, sweet obituary.

III

A man who suffers from the strain
Of unwrit epics in his brain

Can ease the pressure of his grief
With a stub pencil and a leaf.

Old Homer owned no inch of ground,
But sung — and passed his hat around;

No farm, no house, no books, no ink,
But still had divers thoughts to think.

If nothing in the skull abide,
Then nothing helps a man outside;

And what avails a sea of ink
To him who has no thoughts to think?

A Philosopher

Zack Bumstead uster flosserfize
About the ocean and the skies:
An' gab an' gas f'um morn till noon
About the other side the moon;
An' 'bout the natur of the place
Ten miles be-end the end of space.
An' if his wife sh'd ask the crank
Ef he wouldn't kinder try to yank
Hisself out doors an' git some wood
To make her kitchen fire good,
So she c'd bake her beans an' pies,
He'd say, "I've gotter flosserfize."

An' then he'd set an' flosserfize
About the natur an' the size
Of angels' wings, an' think, and gawp,
An' wonder how they made 'em flop.
He'd calkerlate how long a skid

'Twould take to move the sun, he did,
An' if the skid wus strong an' prime,
It couldn't be moved to supper time.
An' w'en his wife 'ud ask the lout
Ef he wouldn' kinder waltz about
An' take a rag an' shoo the flies.
He'd say, "I've gotter flosserfize."

An' then he'd set an' flosserfize
'Bout schemes for fencing in the skies.
Then lettin' out the lots to rent
So's he could make an honest cent.
An' ef he'd find it pooty tough
To borry cash fer fencin' stuff?
An' if 'twere best to take his wealth
An' go to Europe for his health.
Or save his cash till he'd enough
To buy some more of fencin' stufl" —
Then, ef his wife sh'd ask the gump
Ef he wouldn't kinder try to hump
Hisself to tother side the door
So she c'd come an' sweep the floor,
He'd look at her with mournful eyes.
An' say, "I've gotter flosserfize."
An' so he'd set an' flosserfize
'Bout what it wuz held up the skies,
An' how God made this earthly ball
Jest simply out er nawthin' 'tall,
An' 'bout the natur, shape an' form
Of nawthin' thet he made it from.
Then, ef his wife sh'd ask the freak
Ef he wouldn' kinder try to sneak
Out to the barn an' find some aigs,
He'd never move nor lift his laigs
An' never stir nor try to rise
But say, "I've gotter flosserfize."

An' so he'd set an' flosserfize
About the earth an' sea an' skies.
An' scratch his head an' ask the cause
Of w'at there waz before time waz,
An' w'at the universe 'ud do
Bimeby w'en time hed all got through;
An' jest how fur we'd hev to climb
Ef we sh'd travel out er time,

An' ef we'd need w'en we got there
To keep our watches in repair.
Then, ef his wife she'd ask the gawk
Ef he wouldn' kinder try to walk
To where she had the table spread
An' kinder git his stomach fed.
He'd leap for that ar kitchen door
An' say, "W'y didn't you speak afore?"

An' when he'd got his supper et,
He'd set, an' set, an' set, an' set,
An' fold his arms an' shet his eyes,
An' set, an' set, an' flosserfize.

The Dazed Phrenologist

The great phrenologist was dazed
   And lost his usual suavity:
He'd found a man who couldn't be praised,
   Because of his depravity.
"You are a thief," said he; "I fear
You steal, when not prevented."
"But William Shakespeare, he stole deer" —
Said he; " I'm complimented."
"Your temper's bad, you're full of bile,
You rave and fume intensely."
"Oh, yes," said he; "so did Carlyle;
You honor me immensely "
"But you, sir, you are very vain
And weakly egotistic —"
"Oh, yes," said he; "just like Montaigne;
You're very eulogistic."

"You are a cynic." "So was Swift."
"A scoffer." "So was Shelley."
"For lying you've a mighty gift."
"Well, so had Machiavelli."
"But you're conceited, proud, and haut,
A base of pride you're built on."
"Well, so was Michael Angelo
And Dante and John Milton."

"Funds left with you would be misused,
Or I am much mistaken:
Men's trust in you would be abused —"
101

"Why! how like Francis Bacon! —
Well, here's your fee; you've done me proud,
You've ransacked history's pages
To rank me with th' illustrious crowd
Of great men of all ages."

The Three Songs

A poet in the rosy prime
And blithe and dewy morn of time,
When song was natural as breath,
Sent forth his songs to fight with death.

And one he made to please the crowd;
It pleased them, and his praise was loud;
It pleased them greatly for a day,
And then its music died away.

And one he made to please the few;
It lived a century or two;
'Twas sung within the halls of kings,
Then vanished with forgotten things.

And one he made to please himself,
Without a thought of fame or pelf,
But sent it forth with doubt and fears,
And it outlasted all the years.

No other song has vital breath
Through endless time to fight with death,
Than that the singer sings apart
To please his solitary heart.

The Wineless Drunkard

"The air should suffice for his inspiration, and he should be
tipsy with water." — Emerson.

I sing no sot with eyes bloodshot.
    Sing not the staggering throng.
I sing the song of the ginless sot,
    The wineless drunkard's song;
The man who drinks the air as wine,
    Who quaffs with thirsty eye
The dazzle of the tumbling brine,

The glamour of the sky;
The man whom sunlight makes elate,
   Who loves the storm-wind's strife;
I sing the strong inebriate
   Drunk with the wine of life.
Fair dreams his sane delirium throng;
Hear ye the wineless drunkard's song!

The wineless drunkard drinks the mirth
   And music of the morn,
And hears the glad voice of the earth
   Speak in the nestling corn;
He drinks the whiffs from off the meads,
   The spray from salted seas,
The fragrance blown from waving reeds
   And blossomed apple trees.
From many lily-bordered brinks
   Where summer rivulets stray
The gladness of the earth he drinks,
   The freshness of the day;
He drinks, and life grows fair and strong;
Hear ye the wineless drunkard's song!

The incense that the meadow yields
   Within his brain is wrought.
The lushness of the tangled fields
   Is blooming in his thought;
The inland songs of murmurous brooks
   Along their reedy brinks;
The babbling strains from blossomed nooks
   Of tipsy bobolinks;
The breaths that float from bloom and brake,
   The songs from vale and knoll,
Surge in upon his dreams and make
   A summer in his soul.
And lofty is his joy and strong;
Hear ye the wineless drunkard's song!

And when the flower-bells are curled
   Within their dewy rest,
The spirit of the darkling world
   Pervades his pensive breast.
His spirit drinks the peace that lies
   On lakes beneath the moon
Outspread beneath the midnight skies,

Fringed with the wealth of June;
Deep doth the eternal silence press
    Around our eremite,
His soul bathes in the quietness
    And mystery of the night;
And deep his spirit broods and long;
Hear ye the wineless drunkard's song

Mother Putney's "Things"

Old Hiram Putney's house burned down;
And Hiram Putney went to town,
Collected the insurance due,
And made no further hullabaloo;
For Hiram Putney was a man
Built on a stout, substantial plan.

But Mother Putney was a soul
Without heroic self-control,
And if the tears the poor soul shed
In hopeless grief uncomforted
Had been turned on the flames, no doubt
They would have put the fire out;
For Mother Putney dropped her tears
Down the long highway of the years.
For Mother Putney's own heartstrings
Were wound and tied about her "things."

'Tis wide to think and very far
'Twixt Southern Cross and polar star;
And all the sundered worlds were wrought
    Upon a very long, long plan,
And long enough for any thought,
    For the long thought of any man.
But Mother Putney had no far,
Translunar thoughts of sun or star,
Of Neptune's orbit, Saturn's rings, —
She only thought about her "things."

Ah! there are souls whose thoughts are high
As any star within the sky;
Calm, lofty, intellectual kings.
Who have no thought or care for "things";
Who feed, unheeding loss or gain,
On fine abstractions of the brain;

And who would still be unconcerned
If all the homes of men were burned;
There are such souls beneath the sun —
But Mother Putney was not one.

It wrung her soul with dire despair
To think of her lost chinaware;
Whereof she thought if one plate broke
It was misfortune's direst stroke;
If one cup rattled to the floor
The cosmos trembled to its core;
And, if one fragile bowl should smash,
The farthest star would hear the crash.

Her quilts, her pillow-shams, her laces,
Her bric-a-brac, her pots, and vases;
Her tidies on her easy-chairs
That awkward men tore unawares;
Her towels and her table-cloths,
Her carpets kept for years from moths,
All these she cherished with a care,
    A loving care, benignant, mild;
And loved them for the care they were.
    Just as a mother loves a child.
Full many cares were hers. Ah me!
And many things to love had she.

Her wedding dress that once could bound
Her form, but now went half-way round;
Her wedding shoes no longer meet
For her increased expanse of feet;
Her cradle where she rocked young Paul,
Who now is over six feet tall;
The little shoes of baby Ray,
Who travelled such a little way
Through this old world of pain and doubt
That they were only half worn out;
The crib from which her baby May
Took flight into the far away, —
These worthless shoes, these worthless cribs
These worthless aprons, tires, and bibs,
To Mother Putney had a worth
Beyond all treasure-vaults of earth.
'Twas foolish for a burned-up bib,
    'Twas weak to mourn; 'twas weak and wild

To mourn o'er ashes of a crib
     That once had held a dying child.
I know, you wealthy financiers
Primed with the fiscal lore of years,
All deem old Mother Putney rash
And foolish to esteem such trash;
But I, for one, discard your pride.
And stand on Mother Putney's side.
And cannot state my thought too strong,
That she was right and you are wrong;
For in a lost, dead baby's shoe
Are values that you never knew.

Stand back, you intellectual kings.
For Mother Putney and her "things."
Ah, Mother Putney, good and true,
     God keeps his old world in the light
By sending shining souls, like you.
     With deathless love to keep it bright.
'Tis wide to think and very far
'Twixt Southern Cross and polar star;
But God has made no better thing
     In all the stars that rise or set
Than love that grows by cherishing,
     And cannot falter or forget.

On to Washington

Oh, let us march to Washington
          And ask for legislation,
To make the trees grow greenback leaves,
     To make the clouds rain pure milk.
To make nutritious, wooden beeves.
     And strong tenacious cobweb silk,
          For each man in the nation.

Oh, let us march to Washington
          With a polite petition,
That Congress change red sand to meal,
     And make the pie plant bloom with pie;
Or else make all the common weal
     Be satisfied and nourished by
          Spontaneous nutrition.

Oh, let us march to Washington

And ask our legislators
To make pure air a legal food.
   To make all apples without core.
And that all pebbles that are strewed
   Along the misty ocean shore
      Be changed into potatoes.

Oh, let us march to Washington
         And urge with force and reason,
That Congress make all labor crime,
   And abrogate old Adam's fall.
And make all hours dinner time.
   All work unconstitutional,
         And industry high treason.

A Song for Those Who Succeed

A song for those who succeed:
            (You there!)
   You whole successful crew,
Ye men of strong heroic stripe,
   Here is a song for you.
Now who is there here in this whole wide throng
In whose honest ear I can sing my song —
            (Stand up!)

Ah, here's my millionaire:
            (Come here!)
   Good sir, your wealth is great.
And well you have scooped your fortune, man,
   From the loosened grasp of fate.
You have picked up gold as the long years roll,
But while picking up gold you have dropped your soul
            (Go back!)

Ah, here's my wide-browed sage:
            (This way!)
   Five thousand years of lore!
Faith, man, 'tis a goodly heritage,
   But you need a little more.
You have garnered all thoughts from the four winds blown,
But forgotten meantime to think your own;
            (Sit down!)

Ah, here's my artist friend:

(Step up!)
You have given dreams to men,
Yes, a world of dreams you have bodied forth
With chisel, brush, and pen;
But you've lost the meat of the tough world's strife,
And missed the juice of the vintage of life:
(Step down!)

Who's that old woman there?
                    (Sit down!)
    She has no lore or pelf.
And has worked so hard for those she loved
    She has never thought of herself;
Step up, step up in the whole world's view;
Ah, madam, this song is meant for you:
                    (Step up!)

The Wail of the Hack Writer

Ah, dreary is the toil for dull
    And shallow thought — the chaff-choked grain,
That comes from just beneath the skull,
    Not from the brain within the brain.

But all the dull, chaff-nourished tribe
    Must have its favorite food of bran.
And he who writes must let the scribe
    Murder the poet in the man.

Oft must he stem the tides that roll
    From thought's interior deep, and, dead
To their far voices, sell his soul —
    No, not for gold, for bread.

And he must leave the heights that shine
    And hasten down their arduous steeps
To feed the million-throated swine,
    That gulps its garbage and then sleeps.

The Song of the Money Maker

I have smoothed out the hills from the earth
    And heaped them in the sea:
And the buffalo plains I have riddled with trains

That they may fetch dollars to me.
I have beaded the rivers with towns,
    I have hollowed the mountains with mines,
And fastened a girth round the ends of the earth
    That is woven of telegraph lines.

And the dollars come home to their own:
    They know the sound of his voice:
I call my sheep from deep unto deep:
    They flock to their fold and rejoice.
For my ships that sail under the world.
    And my fire steeds out of the West,
Come bearing the spoil of a million's toil
    And the fruit of a world-wide quest.

I stretch me a thousand arms
    That reach to a thousand seas,
And they gather me gain from the land and main
    And heap it at my knees.
But the man with the Book comes close in my wake,
    His feet with swiftness shod.
And the naked man with his savage clan
    Is told of the white man's God.

I am selfish and narrow and gross
    (So say the mawkish crew);
No delicate strain and no fineness of brain
    That goes with the sifted few.
But a man like me must go before
    Ere the artist comes behind;
Through a wild abode I lay the road
    That's paved for the march of mind.

I lead: then the deep-browed sage
    His treasured word indites;
I lead: and the dream-taught bard
    Sits warm by his fire and writes.
The great sky-filling dome
    Through me is reared on high:
And I glean old books into alcoved nooks
    That wisdom may not die.

Mayhap my brain is coarse,
    Mayhap my heart is dry,
And the scholar's scroll and the artist's soul

Are not for such as I.
But a man like me must go before
    Ere the artist comes behind;
Through a wild abode I lay the road
    That's paved for the march of mind.

Arbitration

I

The old blood hungers of a savage prime,
    The tiger hates that since the world began
    Have vexed the lives of battling clan and clan,
Pass with their clash and thunder: but sublime
From out the distance do we hear the chime
    That ushers in the cosmopolitan
    And seer-foretold confederacy of man —
The mightiest offspring of the births of time.

Shall not the nations 'mid their reeking graves
    From war's red bondage hunger to be free
        When they behold two mighty nations stand
With strong hands joined across the sundering waves —
    One, the proud mistress of the empired sea,
        One, her strong daughter of the kingless land?

II

Our sundered nations of the single tongue
    By this great pact of brotherhood shall clear
    The cluttered world of armies. Sword and spear.
Whose clash made music when the world was young,
Must soon upon the rubbish heap be flung; —
    Their clash is discord to the world's tired ear. -
    The first steps of the reign of peace draw near,
The first knell of the death of war has rung.

This is a deed of far and potent reach,
    A deed that makes for universal good:
        By this one deed our sundered nations bind
(Our sundered nations of the single speech),
    Bind by this deed all men in brotherhood,
        And lead the federation of mankind.

The Murder of Maceo

I

Spain dances in her fierce, hyena glee
    Above the murdered form of Maceo.
    Behold the way a coward meets her foe!
But Maceo is victor, and not she;
Hers the defeat and his the victory:
    For when he fell with her assassin blow
    He gained the guerdon only martyrs know;
She crowned a thousand years of infamy.

He stands among the illumined of the years,
    And he has gained his place upon the roll
        Of the undying saviors of the race;
But she, once more, has drowned the world in tears
    And shown how deep a craven nation's soul
        Can wallow in the slime of its disgrace.

II

Doubt not a state was born when Maceo died;
    A new and strong republic in the West
    Sprang into being when he found his rest:
For every blood-drop from his bleeding side
Shall rise, a thousand times re-multiplied^
    An armed man. The wounds upon his breast
    Shall speak like trumpets, and from crest to crest,
And through a wakened world sound far and wide.

Cuba is free; to doubt her freedom now
    Is blackest atheism of the heart:
        Cuba is free — his dying makes her free.
A little while and not a Spanish prow
    The waters round her headlands shall dispart,
        Or vex the peace of her inviolate sea.

Circumstance

A child was born upon a country lane,
    Born with a nature made to mate with throngs;
    And so the morning meadows, glad with songs,
The bobolink's tumultuous refrain,
The babbling music of the glad brooks' strain,

The whip-poor-will that nightly told his wrongs,
And every voice that to the wood belongs.
Smote him with sense of omnipresent pain.

He longed for music of the thunderous street.
The strenuous tumult of the hurrying crowd.
And loathed the voices of his echoing glen;
There in his hated mountain-walled retreat.
Made glorious by many a summer cloud,
He thirsted for the fellowship of men.

II

A child was born within the tall-topt town,
Born with a nature twinned with solitude:
He mixed himself with traffic's strenuous brood.
Went where the world-throngs travel up and down,
But evermore bemoaned fate's iron frown,
And in his heart kept up perpetual feud
With circumstance; and evermore renewed
His natal longing for the wood-paths brown.

And evermore he wandered in his dreams
Through verdurous lanes, 'neath incense-dropping pines,
Far from the town's discordant reel and roar;
And evermore he strolled by lilied streams;
And evermore he dreamed of murmurous vines;
And dreamed of wood-fringed valleys evermore.

The Firefly

That living lantern of the summer night,
That animated torch, the firefly,
A zigzag streak of vital light, goes by,
Himself the luminous torch of his own flight,
Making the odorous darkness dimly bright:
A star, he seems, like to the stars on high.
Making the meadow like another sky, —
A winged star of self-renewing light.

Strong is the soul that in the meadow land
In midnight hours when the envenomed dark
Enrobes the spirit with its heavy gloom,
Can, like the firefly, its wings expand
And light with its own self- engendered spark,
Self-luminant, the midnight of its doom.

The Word

The Word Divine vouchsafed by God to man
   Is uttered through the years of many an age;
   And there are lips touched with the prophet's rage
To-day, as there have been since time began:
Not to a far-off patriarchal clan,
   To Idumean or Judean sage,
   Did God alone indite a sacred page
In narrow lands, 'twixt Beersheba and Dan.

God's voice is wandering now on every wind
   And speaks its message to the tuned ear;
    And here are holy groves and sacred streams;
On every hill are sacred altars shrined;
   And prophets tell their message now and here;
    Young men see visions and old men dream dreams.

The Book of Job

Great song of gloom, a broken voice of tears
   Blown from afar, from deeps of time upcast;
   A dirge from out the dimness of the Vast;
A wail that trembles with its weight of fears;
A voice discordant with the chiming spheres
   The choric star-song of that distant past;
   A cry for succor on the midnight blast,
A night song from the morning of the years!

Joy has forever been the smiling guest
   Wherever human hearths or homes have stood,
    A smiling guest since first the years began;
But these far wails forevermore attest
   That Sorrow, too, proclaims her sisterhood.
    Her everlasting sisterhood with Man.

The Artist

The artist wrongs his art to talk of art;
   He is no babbler. He is of the few
   Inevitable, unconscious souls who *do,*
And what he does is an incorporate part
Of that great work the universal heart
   Has ever purposed since the world was new.

Let him not babble with the babbling crew,
The wrangling tonguesters in the public mart.

Through him the impatient silence of old time,
    Its inarticulate yearning finds a tongue;
        Through him the voiceless latencies are heard:
He need not justify himself.   Sublime
    Through his surrendered lips new songs are sung,
        The Voice of the Great Vastness speaks its word.

A Shred of Kelp

A shred of kelp was tossed upon the breast
    Of the great sea; a plaything for the blast,
    A plaything for the multitudinous, vast,
And never-resting sea. From crest to crest
Of the white waves 'twas shouldered without rest,
    Past summer isles and wintry headlands past.
    Drenched by the tide- sweep, by the waves upcast,
Tossed by all seas between the East and West.

What is our life in the on-rushing sweep
    Of the great current? Ah, the sea is wide
        And one man's life is very small, ah me! —
A shred of kelp on the imperious deep,
    A shred of kelp on the tumultuous tide
        That rolls from out the vastness of the sea.

www.ingramcontent.com/pod-product-compliance
Lightning Source LLC
Chambersburg PA
CBHW031536040426
42445CB00010B/571